COLLECTIONS

Read-Aloud Anthology
Grade 3

Harcourt

Orlando Boston Dallas Chicago San Diego

Visit *The Learning Site!*

www.harcourtschool.com

For permission to reprint copyrighted material, grateful acknowledgment is made to the following sources:

Atheneum Books for Young Readers, an imprint of Simon & Schuster Children's Publishing Division: "Since Hanna Moved Away" from *If I Were in Charge of the World and Other Worries* by Judith Viorst. Text copyright © 1981 by Judith Viorst.
August House Publishers, Inc.: "The Bat" and "The Theft of a Smell" from *Twenty-Two Splendid Tales to Tell From Around the World*, Volume Two by Pleasant DeSpain. Text © 1979, 1990, 1994 by Pleasant DeSpain.
Boyds Mills Press, Inc.: Big Moon Tortilla by Joy Cowley. Text copyright © 1998 by Joy Cowley. "The Three Little Pigs" from *Once Upon a Bedtime Story*, retold by Jane Yolen. Text copyright © 1997 by Jane Yolen.
Candlewick Press Inc., Cambridge, MA: Saturday Night at the Dinosaur Stomp by Carol Diggory Shields, illustrated by Scott Nash. Text copyright © 1997 by Carol Diggory Shields; illustrations copyright © 1997 by Scott Nash.
Children's Television Workshop, New York, NY: "Figuring Out What's On Your Pet's Mind" by Tracey Randinelli from *Contact Kids* Magazine, September 1998. Text copyright 1998 by Children's Television Workshop.
The Literary Executor of Leonard Clark: "Good Company" by Leonard Clark.
CRICKET Magazine: "One Little Can" by David LaRochelle from *Cricket* Magazine, April 1997, Vol. 24, No. 8. Text © 1997 by David LaRochelle. "Fish, Flowers, and Fruit" by Joyce Sidman from *Cricket* Magazine, July 1998, Vol. 25, No. 11. Text © 1998 by Joyce Sidman.
Free To Be Foundation, Inc.: "Atalanta" from *Free to Be . . . You and Me* by Betty Miles. Text copyright © 1973 by Free to Be Foundation, Inc.
Harcourt, Inc.: "Doing Dishes" from *Canto familiar* by Gary Soto. Text copyright © 1995 by Gary Soto.
HarperCollins Publishers: "De Koven" and "Rudolph Is Tired of the City" from *Bronzeville Boys and Girls* by Gwendolyn Brooks. Text copyright © 1956 by Gwendolyn Brooks Blakely. "Helping" from *Where the Sidewalk Ends* by Shel Silverstein. Text copyright © 1974 by Evil Eye Music, Inc.
Highlights for Children, Inc., Columbus, OH: "A Measure of Spice" by Kelly Musselman from *Highlights for Children* Magazine, September 1998. Text copyright © 1998 by Highlights for Children, Inc.
Virginia Kidd Agency, Inc.: Aurora Means Dawn by Scott Russell Sanders. Text copyright © 1989 by Scott Russell Sanders. Published by Simon & Schuster Books for Young Readers.
Alfred A. Knopf, Inc.: "The Clever Warthog" from *Golden Shadows, Flying Hooves* by George B. Schaller. Text copyright © 1973 by George B. Schaller.
Maxine Kumin: The Microscope by Maxine Kumin. Text copyright © 1968 by Maxine Kumin.
Libraries Unlimited, Inc. (800-237-6124): "Why Birds Are Never Hungry" from *Folk Stories of the Hmong: Peoples of Laos, Thailand, and Vietnam* by Norma J. Livo and Dia Cha. Text copyright © 1991 by Libraries Unlimited, Inc.
Modern Curriculum Press, Inc.: "The Power Shovel" from *The Day Is Dancing* by Rowena Bastin Bennett. Text © 1968 by Modern Curriculum Press, Inc., an imprint of Pearson Learning.
Morrow Junior Books, a division of William Morrow and Company, Inc.: Johnny Appleseed, retold by Steven Kellogg. Copyright © 1988 by Steven Kellogg. "How the Girl Taught the Coyotes to Sing Harmony" from *The Girl Who Loved Coyotes: Stories of the Southwest* by Nancy Wood. Text copyright © 1995 by Nancy Wood.
Orchard Books, New York: The Thing That Bothered Farmer Brown by Teri Sloat, illustrated by Nadine Bernard Westcott. Text copyright © 1995 by Teri Sloat; illustrations copyright © 1995 by Nadine Bernard Westcott.
Dick Orr: "A Billion Baseballs" from *Bailey Bought a Billion Baseballs* by Dick Orr.
Oxford University Press: "The Key of the Kingdom" (anonymous) from *The Oxford Treasury of Children's Poems* by Michael Harrison and Christopher Stuart-Clark. Originally published in the United States of America by Oxford University Press, 1988.
Random House Children's Books, a division of Random House, Inc.: Half-Chicken by Alma Flor Ada. Text copyright © 1995 by Alma Flor Ada.
Lawrence Reeves: Limericks from *The Little Book of Limericks*, compiled by Warren Lyfick.
David Roth: "Nine Gold Medals" by David Roth. Text © 1988 by David Roth.
Scholastic Inc.: "The Billy Goat and the Vegetable Garden" from *Señor Cat's Romance and Other Favorite Stories from Latin America*, retold by Lucía M. González. Text copyright © 1997 by Lucía M. González. Published by Scholastic Press, a division of Scholastic Inc. "Garrett A. Morgan" from *Five Notable Inventors*, a Hello Reader! by Wade Hudson. Text copyright © 1995 by Wade Hudson. Published by Cartwheel Books, a division of Scholastic Inc. "Amelia Earhart" from *My First Book of Biographies: Great Men and Women Every Child Should Know* by Jean Marzollo. Text copyright © 1994 by Jean Marzollo. Published by Cartwheel Books, a division of Scholastic Inc. "Young Koko" from *Koko's Story* by Dr. Francine Patterson. Text copyright © 1987 by The Gorilla Foundation.
Simon & Schuster Books for Young Readers, Simon & Schuster Children's Publishing Division: Someplace Else by Carol P. Saul. Text copyright © 1995 by Carol P. Saul.
Simon & Schuster, Inc.: "The Eagle Has Landed" and "Margaret of New Orleans" from *The Children's Book of America*, edited by William J. Bennett. Text copyright © 1998 by William J. Bennett.
SPIDER Magazine: "Teddy's Bear" by Janeen R. Adil from *Spider* Magazine, Vol. 5, No. 5. Text © 1998 by Janeen R. Adil. "Old Crocodile" by Sydnie Meltzer Kleinhenz from *Spider* Magazine, Vol. 5, No. 2. Text © 1998 by Sydnie Meltzer Kleinhenz. "A Scrap and a Robe" by Myrina D. McCullough from *Spider* Magazine, Vol. 5, No. 2. Text © 1998 by Myrina D. McCullough.
Viking Penguin, a division of Penguin Putnam Inc.: "The Country Mouse and the City Mouse" from *Aesop's Fables*. Text copyright © 1981 by Viking Penguin, Inc.
Workman Publishing Co., Inc., New York: "America, the Beautiful Home of Dinosaurs" from *Bone Poems* by Jeff Moss. Text copyright © 1997 by Jeff Moss.

Reading Aloud to Children

by Dr. Dorothy S. Strickland

The children sit in rapt attention. They are engrossed as they listen to a story read with enthusiasm by Janine White, their teacher. There is a pause as Janine appears to think out loud: "I wonder what will happen next." Several responses are met by her reply: "Let's read on and see." Later, Janine makes a brief explanatory comment about a word that might be puzzling to the children. Now and then she injects a well-placed question or comment to focus the children's attention on a key aspect of the story: "How do you think the boy feels now? What makes you think so?" "Well, that was certainly a surprise!" These are kept brief so that the flow of the story is never interrupted. Were this an informational book, however, Janine and her students might linger on a single page for several minutes, savoring new concepts and sharing ideas, before moving on. Small wonder that reading aloud in this classroom is a favorite part of the day.

Read-aloud time serves many purposes. Children's exposure to and enjoyment of good quality literature has long been recognized as key to building positive attitudes about reading. In recent years, however, sharing stories, informational books, and poetry with children in this way has become increasingly valued for its cognitive contribution to children's literacy development.

Following are some of the key contributions of read-aloud time to the literacy program and some tips for making the most of this valuable asset to the curriculum.

Why Read Aloud?

- **Read-aloud time builds children's background knowledge.** Select books that expand knowledge of the world as well as their imaginations. Keep in mind that young children's listening comprehension exceeds their reading comprehension, so read material that stretches them well beyond what they can read on their own levels. Read-aloud time can be a key component of content-area studies. Listening to and discussing informational books that deal with social studies and science themes can insure that all children have access to information that some may have difficulty reading independently.

- **Read-aloud time helps children's understanding of text structures.** Select from a wide range of material. Keep in mind that there is variety even within the narrative form. Children who have been exposed to a variety of types of stories develop a keen sense of the differences among them. For example, they become familiar with simple narrative tales, with cumulative tales that form a particular pattern, and with mystery stories with problems to solve and clues to help solve them. Exposure to poetry and various forms of informational texts also helps children understand the nature of various written forms. Familiarity with a variety of text structures serves as an aid to children's reading comprehension and to their writing as well.

- **Read-aloud time provides important opportunities for students to respond to literature in a variety of ways.** Build response to literature into the read-aloud program. Very often, the response to a poem or story will be very brief and quite informal. Sometimes Janine simply closes the book and queries: "Observations?" The children may respond verbally to the selection as a whole or to any part they wish: That story reminds me of ___; I liked the part when ___; I was really scared until ___; I learned that ___. Sometimes Janine records their responses on a chart to be reread and added to after subsequent readings. Children need opportunities to respond in a variety of ways. Group discussion, writing, drawing, drama, and movement are among the many ways students might respond to literature read aloud.

- **Read-aloud time offers students opportunities to build listening comprehension skills.** Choose literature that captures children's interests and attention. Students must experience a kind of engagement with literature if they are to develop their abilities to comprehend, respond, and apply what they hear and learn. Children's first experiences with this kind of engagement are through read-aloud time, when they become so involved with a selection that they truly experience it. These experiences serve as the basis for learning to interpret and think critically about what is read.

Some Tips for Reading Aloud to Children

1. Read aloud on a regular basis.
2. Avoid scheduling the read-aloud time at the end of the day, when it is more likely to be omitted.
3. Read with expression. Show your own interest and enthusiasm for the selection.
4. Early in the year, establish rules of behavior during read-aloud time. Do this with students, emphasizing the need to respect everyone's right to enjoy the story. Let group pressure do the rest.

Contents

Stories

Realistic Fiction

Myths and Fables

Folktales

Songs

Poems

Nonfiction

Stories

The Microscope

by Maxine Kumin

PURPOSE FOR LISTENING: to gain information

READ-ALOUD TIP: Emphasize the rhyming words in this biographical tale.

Anton Leeuwenhoek was Dutch. He sold pincushions, cloth, and such.

The waiting townsfolk fumed and fussed, as Anton's dry goods gathered dust.

He worked, instead of tending store, at grinding special lenses for a microscope.

Instead of working in his store, what does Anton Leeuwenhoek do?

Some of the things he looked at were: mosquitoes' wings, the hairs of sheep, the legs of lice, the skin of people, dogs, and mice; ox eyes, spiders' spinning gear, fishes' scales, a little smear of his own blood, and best of all, the unknown, busy, very small bugs that swim and bump and hop inside a simple water drop.

Impossible! most Dutchmen said.

This Anton's crazy in the head. He says he's seen a horsefly's brain.

We ought to ship him off to Spain. He says the water that we drink is full of bugs. He's mad, we think!

They called him domkop, which means dope. That's how we got the microscope.

---

1. **What did you learn about Anton Leeuwenhoek?**
   (Possible response: He spent his time grinding lenses and looking at things under his microscope.)

2. **Why do you think the townspeople thought Anton Leeuwenhoek was wasting his time?** (Responses will vary.)

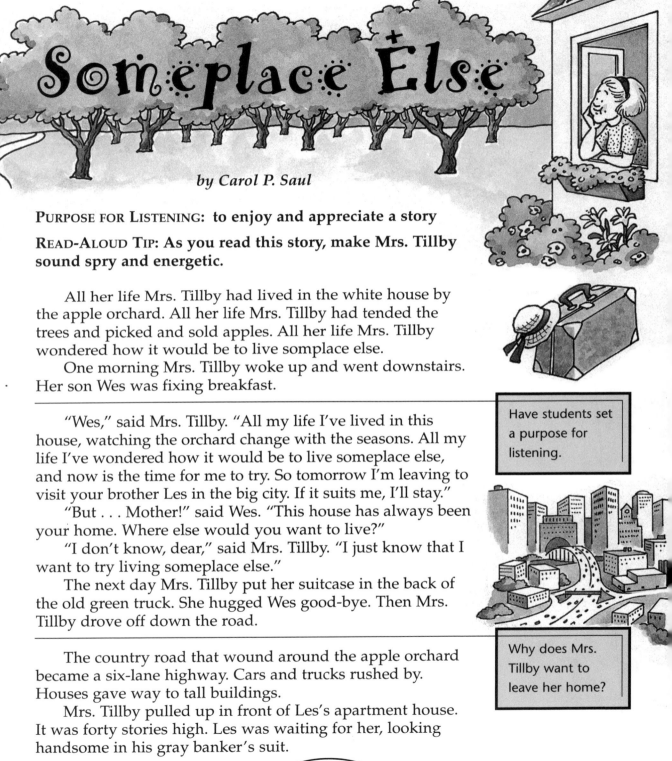

Someplace Else

by Carol P. Saul

PURPOSE FOR LISTENING: to enjoy and appreciate a story

READ-ALOUD TIP: As you read this story, make Mrs. Tillby sound spry and energetic.

All her life Mrs. Tillby had lived in the white house by the apple orchard. All her life Mrs. Tillby had tended the trees and picked and sold apples. All her life Mrs. Tillby wondered how it would be to live somplace else.

One morning Mrs. Tillby woke up and went downstairs. Her son Wes was fixing breakfast.

"Wes," said Mrs. Tillby. "All my life I've lived in this house, watching the orchard change with the seasons. All my life I've wondered how it would be to live someplace else, and now is the time for me to try. So tomorrow I'm leaving to visit your brother Les in the big city. If it suits me, I'll stay."

"But . . . Mother!" said Wes. "This house has always been your home. Where else would you want to live?"

"I don't know, dear," said Mrs. Tillby. "I just know that I want to try living someplace else."

The next day Mrs. Tillby put her suitcase in the back of the old green truck. She hugged Wes good-bye. Then Mrs. Tillby drove off down the road.

The country road that wound around the apple orchard became a six-lane highway. Cars and trucks rushed by. Houses gave way to tall buildings.

Mrs. Tillby pulled up in front of Les's apartment house. It was forty stories high. Les was waiting for her, looking handsome in his gray banker's suit.

> Have students set a purpose for listening.

> Why does Mrs. Tillby want to leave her home?

"Welcome to the city, Mother!" said Les, kissing her on the top of her head. "I know you're going to love it here!"

"Thank you, dear," said Mrs. Tillby. She stood on tiptoe to reach his cheek. "It looks that way to me!"

Mrs. Tillby was happy in the city. She went to museums and theaters and stores and restaurants. She saw all sorts of people and tried all kinds of food. At night, from her bedroom window, she could see the lights of the city shining brighter than the stars.

But after a few weeks she wanted to move on.

"I can see why you love city life, Les," said Mrs. Tillby, "with all the hustle and bustle, and so much to see and do. But it doesn't feel like home to me, so I want to try living someplace else."

"Oh, Mother," said Les, "stay a while longer. You haven't seen half of the city."

Mrs. Tillby patted Les's hand.

"You're a dear boy," she said, "and a lovely host. But tomorrow I'm leaving to visit your sister Tess at the seashore. If it suits me, I'll stay."

The next day Mrs. Tillby put her suitcase in the back of the old green truck. She hugged Les good-bye and set off toward the highway.

Soon the six-lane highway thinned out. The tall buildings gave way to houses again. Seagulls swooped and called overhead. Mrs. Tillby smelled salt in the air.

Mrs. Tillby pulled up to Tess's house. It stood on stilts at the edge of the ocean. Tess was waiting for her, wearing a fisherman's yellow slicker. The twins were waiting too.

"Grandma! Grandma!" they cried.

"Welcome to the seashore, Mother!" said Tess. "You'll just love it here!"

> Where does Mrs. Tillby go after she has seen the city? Do you think she'll be happy there?

"Thank you, dear," said Mrs. Tillby, hugging everyone at once. "I'm sure I will."

Mrs. Tillby did like the house on stilts. From her window she could see far out over the ocean. She spent hours gathering shells with the twins and helped Tess cook

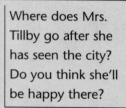

fresh fish and chowder for dinner. Every evening Mrs. Tillby went for a barefoot walk along the shore. At night the sound of the waves lulled her to sleep.

But after a few weeks she needed to move on.

"I understand why you love living by the shore, Tess," said Mrs. Tillby. "The sea is always changing, and the air is ever so clear. But it doesn't feel like home to me, so I want to try living someplace else."

"Oh, Mother," said Tess, "you haven't been here long enough. Wait until you see the wild waves at neap tide!"

Mrs. Tillby patted her hand.

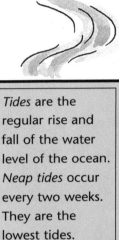

Tides are the regular rise and fall of the water level of the ocean. *Neap tides* occur every two weeks. They are the lowest tides.

"You're a dear girl," she said, "and you've made me very welcome. But tomorrow I'm leaving to visit your brother Jackson in the mountains. If it suits me, I'll stay."

The next day Mrs. Tillby hugged Tess and the twins. She put her suitcase in the back of the old green truck and drove off down the road.

The road narrowed and became twisty. Sand dunes gave way to hills, and hills to mountains. Hawks wheeled above her.

Mrs. Tillby pulled up to Jackson's house. It was made of stone and sat on the edge of a cliff. Jackson came out to greet her in his thick woolen lumberjacket. He wrapped his mother in a big bear hug.

"Welcome to the mountains, Mother!" he said. "You're going to love it here!"

"Thank you, dear," said Mrs. Tillby, adjusting her glasses. "I can't imagine anything nicer."

Mrs. Tillby loved the mountains and the smell of pine that filled the air. Every night she lit a fire in the great stone fireplace. Winter came, and snow fell like a thick white blanket. Jackson's wife taught her how to ski.

But after a few weeks she felt like moving on.

"I know why you love the mountains, Jackson," said Mrs. Tillby. "You can see for miles around, and there is more wildlife than I ever dreamed of. But it just doesn't feel like home to me. I'm going to try someplace else."

"Oh, Mother," said Jackson, "at least stay the winter. And you must see the mountains in early spring."

Mrs. Tillby patted his hand.

"You're a dear boy," she said, "and you've treated me like a guest. But I am leaving tomorrow."

"But Mother Tillby," said Jackson's wife, whose name was Bess. "Where will you go? You're tired of the orchard, you've tried the mountains and the seashore, and big-city life doesn't suit you. What is left?"

"I don't know, dear," said Mrs. Tillby. "There must be someplace else."

The next day Mrs. Tillby put her suitcase in the back of the old green truck. She hugged Jackson and his wife, and drove down the mountain road.

Mrs. Tillby tried living in lots of places. She stayed in a cabin by a lake and in a fire tower high above a forest. She stayed in an adobe hut in the middle of the desert. She even spent time on a riverboat!

> Why do you think Mrs. Tillby leaves every place she visits?

But everywhere she went, it was the same. Mrs. Tillby was always happy at first. After a few weeks she always wanted to move on.

One morning Mrs. Tillby put her suitcase in the back of the old green truck for the last time. Wearily she set off back toward the apple orchard.

"All my life," said Mrs. Tillby as she drove, "I've wanted to live someplace else. Now I've tried all kinds of places, and nothing suits me."

Mrs. Tillby had almost reached the road that led to the orchard when she came to a crossroads. There, parked at a gas station, she saw a shiny silver trailer. FOR SALE read the sign in the window. Mrs. Tillby leaped out of the old green truck. She asked to see the inside of the trailer.

The silver trailer had a cozy bedroom, a tiny bathroom, and a kitchen that folded out of sight.

Mrs. Tillby bought it on the spot.

Now, every few weeks, Mrs. Tillby sets off in the old green truck with the shiny silver trailer attached behind. Sometimes she visits Les in the city, or Tess at the seashore, or Jackson and his wife in the mountains. Sometimes she stays in other places. And in the autumn Mrs. Tillby goes back to the white house by the orchard to help Wes pick and sell apples.

Mrs. Tillby is always home, and she is always someplace else.

---

1. How does Mrs. Tillby find just the right place to live?
(Possible response: She finds the right place by buying a trailer and moving every few weeks.)

2. Of all the places Mrs. Tillby visited, which place would you like to live in? (Responses will vary.)

Big Moon Tortilla [1]

by Joy Cowley

PURPOSE FOR LISTENING: to enjoy and appreciate a story

READ-ALOUD TIP: Vary the pace at which you read this story to reflect the main character's mounting frustration and her grandmother's calm advice.

[1] (tor-TEE-uh)

By the time Marta Enos had finished her homework, the sky was orange with sunset, and a fussing wind was blowing across the desert. Marta Enos opened her window and looked outside.

In the cookhouse, Grandmother was making tortillas for the church supper. She slapped them into large circles and tossed them onto the iron plate over the mesquite (muh-SKEET) fire. Grandmother's big moon tortillas were the best in the world!

Have students set a purpose for listening.

A *tortilla* is a round, flat Mexican bread made from flour or cornmeal.

The head of Marta Enos was filled with the knowing of fresh tortillas. Oh, that sweet, crisp, little-bit-burnt smell! It went to Marta's stomach, which rumbled and growled, and then on down to her feet, making her toes twitch towards the cookhouse.

The legs of Marta Enos would not wait another minute. They were in such a hurry to run to the cookhouse that they knocked over Marta's table, and that is when a disaster happened.

The homework papers with their neat writing and beautiful drawings went out the window and onto the breath of the fussing wind.

The wind huffed the papers high into the air. Then, with a little cough, it spread them over the village.

The legs of Marta Enos were sorry for their mistake, and they ran out to chase the homework papers, which slipped and slid like kites without string.

But the dogs, too, were chasing. Leaping into the air, they barked to each other, A game! A game!

In no time at all, the beautiful homework papers were torn and chewed into trash.

The second disaster happened when Marta tried to pull a page away from a puppy. Her glasses fell off, and she stepped on them. One arm of her glasses broke in half.

What causes Marta's two disasters? How do you think she feels about this?

She did not smell tortillas anymore. Her head was filled up to her eyes with grief and tears as hot as chili peppers. Ruined homework! Broken glasses! Marta Enos ran to Grandmother.

Grandmother left her tortillas and sat down, as big as a bed and warm from the cooking. As she smoothed Marta's hair with her floured hands, she said, "Hush! Hush! If you cry so much you'll put out the fire."

"The dogs ate my homework, and I can't see to do any more!" Marta sobbed.

Grandmother rocked her. "Little problems," she said. "Too small for a big rainstorm. We'll repair your eyeglasses."

But the tears of Marta Enos still ran through her eyes and nose and made hiccups in her throat. So Grandmother sang to her an old healing song, and with the healing song there was a story.

When we have a problem we must choose what we will be. Sometimes it is good to be a tree, to stand up tall in the desert and look all ways at once. Sometimes it is best to be a rock, to sit very still, seeing nothing and saying nothing.

"Sometimes when you have a problem, you have to be a strong mountain lion, fierce and ready to fight for what is right."

"Sometimes the wisest thing is to be an eagle and fly. When the eagle is high up, it sees how small the earth is. It sees how small the problem is, and it laughs and laughs."

Grandmother wound some tape around the arm of the glasses. She put the glasses back on the nose and ears of Marta Enos. "That should be OK until we get them fixed," she said. "Now, one tortilla before supper?"

Grandmother pinched a ball of dough and slapped it between her hands, flip-flap, flip-flap, flip-flap. When it was as big and pale as a rising full moon, she dropped it onto the iron plate above the red-hot coals of the fire. Ah, the smell as the tortilla bubbled and browned!

"I have decided," said Marta Enos, her legs doing a tortilla dance, "I am going to be the eagle."

Grandmother nodded. "That is very wise," she said, turning the tortilla over. "Fly high and laugh. Then come back, and do your homework."

---

1. **What does Marta learn about solving problems from listening to her grandmother's story?** (Possible response: Marta learns that there are many ways you can look at a problem in order to solve it.)

2. **Have you ever had a problem like Marta's? How did you solve it?** (Responses will vary.)

Saturday Night at the Dinosaur Stomp

by Carol Diggory Shields
illustrated by Scott Nash

PURPOSE FOR LISTENING: to enjoy and appreciate a story

READ-ALOUD TIP: Emphasize the rhythm as well as the rhyming words as you read this fantasy tale.

Have students set a purpose for listening.

Word went out 'cross the prehistoric slime:
"Hey, dinosaurs, it's rock 'n' roll time!
Slick back your scales and get ready to romp
On Saturday night at the **Dinosaur Stomp!**"

How do the dinosaurs get ready for their party?

By the lava beds and the tar pit shore,
On the mountain top and the rain forest floor,
Dinosaurs scrubbed their necks and nails.
They brushed their teeth and curled their tails.
Then — ready, set, go — they trampled and tromped,
Making dinosaur tracks for the Dinosaur Stomp.

Plesiosaurus (PLEE-zee-uh-saw-russ) paddled up with a splash,
A pterodactyl (tair-uh-DAK-til) family flew in for the bash.
Protoceratops (pro-toe-SER-uh-tops) brought along her eggs,
Diplodocus (dih-PLOD-uh-kuss) plodded on big fat legs.
A batch of bouncing babies followed Mama Maiasaur
    (MY-uh-sawr).
The last time she counted, she had twenty-four.

The old ones gathered in a gossiping bunch,
Sitting and sipping sweet Swampwater Punch.
Dinosaurs giggled and shuffled and stared,
Ready to party, but a little bit scared.

> Why do you think
> the dinosaurs are
> a little bit scared?

Then Iguanodon (ig-WAN-uh-don) shouted, "One, two, **three!**"
Started up the band by waving a tree.
Brachio- (BRAK-ee-o), Super-, and Ultrasaurus
    (UHL-truh-saw-russ)
Sang, "Doo-bop-a-loo-bop," all in a chorus.
Ankylosaurus (an-KILE-uh-saw-russ) drummed on his hard-
    shelled back,
Boomalacka boomalacka! **Whack! Whack! Whack!**

Pentaceratops (PEN-tuh-ser-uh-tops) stood up to perform
And blasted a tune on his favorite horn.
They played in rhythm, they sang in rhyme,
Dinosaur music in dinosaur time!

Duckbill thought he'd take a chance:
Asked Allosaurus (AL-uh-saw-russ) if she'd like to dance.
Tarchia (TAR-kee-uh) winked at a stegosaur (STEG-uh-sawr)
    she liked.
They danced together, spike to spike.
The Triassic Twist and the Brontosaurus (BRON-tuh-saw-russ) Bump,
The Raptor Rap and Jurassic Jump.

Tyrannosaurus Rex (tie-RAN-uh-saw-russ REX) led a
  conga line.
Carnosaurs (KAR-nuh-sawrz) capered close behind.
They rocked and rolled, they twirled and tromped.
There never was a party like the **Dinosaur Stomp.**

The nighttime sky began to glow.
Volcanoes put on a fireworks show.
The ground was rocking — it started to shake.
Those dinosaurs danced up the first earthquake!

The party went on — it was so outrageous,
They stayed up well past the late Cretaceous (kreh-TAY-shuss).

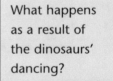

What happens
as a result of
the dinosaurs'
dancing?

When the Cenozoic (sen-uh-ZO-ik) dawned they were tired
  and beat.
They yawned big yawns and put up their feet.
And they're *still* asleep, snoring deep in the swamp.
But they'll be back . . . next **Dinosaur Stomp!**

---

1. **According to the story, where are the dinosaurs now?**
   (Possible response: They are sleeping deep in the swamp.)

2. **What did you learn about dinosaurs from listening to
   this story?** (Possible response: There were many kinds of dinosaurs,
   such as the plesiosaurus, the protoceratops, the maiasaur, the
   pterodactyl, the diplodocus, and the pentaceratops.)

THE THING THAT BOTHERED FARMER BROWN

by Teri Sloat
illustrated by Nadine Bernard Westcott

PURPOSE FOR LISTENING: to identify rhymes and repeated sounds

READ-ALOUD TIP: Encourage children to join in on the repeated lines of this cumulative rhyming story.

Have students set a purpose for listening.

"The animals are bedded down;
My chores are done," said Farmer Brown.
And as he stretched, the sun went down.

But tails and feathers swished the ground
At something flying round and round
With a tiny, whiny, humming sound.

The farmer ate his soup and bread,
Put his nightshirt on, and climbed into bed.
He pulled up the sheet and the worn-out spread
And, closing his eyes, he laid down his head.

But something bothered Farmer Brown;
Something was flying round and round
With a tiny, whiny, humming sound.

The farmer gave a **SWAT** at the wall

That roused the horse asleep in the stall
And the weary donkey, Butterball.
But it didn't stop the humming at all.

The old horse neighed,
The donkey brayed . . .

But the thing annoying Farmer Brown
Was something flying round and round
With a tiny, whiny, humming sound.

His newspaper hit the wall
With a **WHACK**

What is annoying Farmer Brown while he's trying to sleep? What does he do about it?

That upset the doves roosting in the back
And the dairy cows marked white and black.
But the humming just kept coming back.

The doves cooed,
The cows mooed,
The old horse neighed,
The donkey brayed . . .

But the thing disturbing Farmer Brown
Was something flying round and round
With a tiny, whiny, humming sound.

The farmer gave a **SNAP** with his sheet

That startled the grumpy old goat to his feet
And made the hens flutter, scattering wheat.
But the humming barely missed a beat.

How do you think
Farmer Brown is
feeling now?

The old goat bucked,
The chickens clucked,
The doves cooed,
The cows mooed,
The old horse neighed,
The donkey brayed . . .

But the thing exhausting Farmer Brown
Was something flying round and round
With a tiny, whiny, humming sound.

This time he stood still
While the humming came near.
He lifted his hand as it lit on his ear,
Gave a **SMACK**
To his noggin' so loud and so clear
That the old dog and cat
Couldn't help overhear.

Why does Farmer
Brown hit himself
on the head?

The cat yowled,
The dog howled,
The old goat bucked,
The chickens clucked,
The doves cooed,
The cows mooed,
The old horse neighed,
The donkey brayed . . .

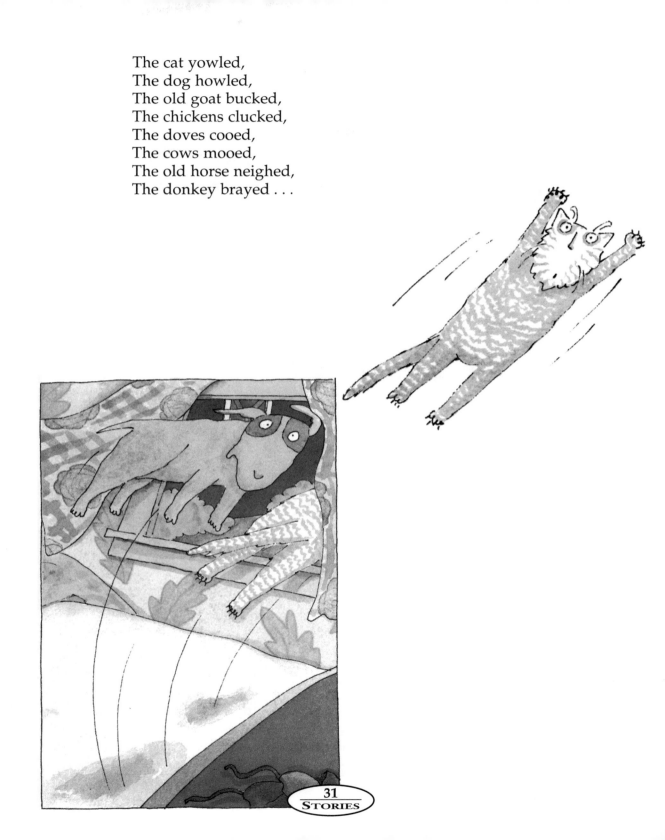

But the farmer **SNORED!**

What do you think will happen next?

The animals slowly settled down
With heads tucked in and
Tails curled round.
The entire farm was sleeping sound

When they heard it flying round and round . . .

That tiny, whiny, humming sound.

1. **What do you think will happen when the animals hear the humming sound?** (Possible response: The annoying humming sound will keep them awake.)

2. **Name some of the rhyming words or repeated sounds you remember from the story.** (Possible responses: Brown/down; ground/round/sound; bread/bed/spread/head; wall/stall/Butterball/all; back/black; sheet/feet/wheat/beat; near/ear/clear/overhear; bucked/clucked; cooed/mooed; neighed/brayed; yowled/howled)

Realistic Fiction

One Little Can

by David LaRochelle

PURPOSE FOR LISTENING: to respond appropriately to questions

READ-ALOUD TIP: Use a different voice for each character.

Rachel scowled in disgust as she walked to the school bus stop. Her neighborhood looked like a junkyard. The sidewalk was littered with newspapers and candy wrappers. The front door to Lee's Grocery was covered with ugly graffiti. It was spring, but instead of green grass and flowers, the yards seemed to be sprouting broken branches and trash.

"Yuck!" Rachel said as she brought her foot back to kick a soda can off the curb. Then she changed her mind, picked the can up, and tossed it into a litter basket on the corner. She hurried to meet her friends at the bus stop.

> How does Rachel feel while she is walking to the bus stop? How do her feelings affect what she does when she sees the soda can?

Mr. Lee scowled as he looked out his grocery store window. "Hmph," he said as the girl passed by. She's probably another troublemaker, he thought. One of those kids who spray-painted graffiti all over my door. Kids today are just no good.

To confirm his suspicion, the girl stepped back to kick a piece of garbage into the street. What she did next, though, surprised him. She bent down, picked up the old can, and dropped it into a trash can.

That's a switch, thought Mr. Lee.

> What do you think Mr. Lee will do next?

All morning as he unboxed soup cans and cereal boxes, he kept picturing that girl. At noon, when he walked to the corner to mail a letter, he noticed the litter that had piled up in front of his store. He thought of that girl again, then got a broom and started sweeping the walk.

Mrs. Polansky peered out from between the window blinds in her living room. A crumpled sheet of newspaper blew into her yard and got snagged on a rosebush. She hated

REALISTIC FICTION

living across the street from Lee's Grocery. Customers were always dropping their trash in front of the store, and invariably it would blow into her yard.

Maybe I should write a letter to the city council, she thought, or call the mayor. If Mr. Lee is going to let his store be such an eyesore, maybe it should be shut down.

Just then Mr. Lee walked out his door. Mrs. Polansky quickly shut the blinds, but when she peeked out again, he was sweeping up the trash on his sidewalk.

That's a change, thought Mrs. Polansky.

A few minutes later, when she went to let her cat out, she noticed that the stray newspaper had unsnagged itself from her rosebush and was tumbling into the next yard. She caught a glimpse of Ms. Sinclaire, her neighbor, frowning at her from the porch.

Mrs. Polansky looked around at her own unkempt yard.

"Well, Fluffy," she said to her cat, "Mr. Lee isn't the only one who can do a bit of outdoor spring cleaning."

She went inside and got her work gloves and a trash bag.

When Rachel got off the school bus that afternoon, the first thing she noticed was the woman planting geraniums around the edges of her front walk. A fat gray cat was swatting at a butterfly that flitted among the bright red blossoms. Hadn't that yard been strewn with dead branches and soggy newspapers this morning? Several other yards looked tidier, too. She even spotted a pair of crocuses peeking up from a freshly raked garden.

When she passed Lee's Grocery, Mr. Lee was out front painting his door the color of a spring sky. He smiled at her as she walked by.

> How do you think Rachel feels now? Explain.

Maybe my neighborhood doesn't look so bad after all, Rachel thought. She knelt down and picked up a lone candy bar wrapper, slam-dunked it into the litter basket, and sang out loud the rest of the way home.

Rachel throws an empty can into the trash. How does this change her neighborhood? (Possible response: It starts a chain of good deeds that cleans up her neighborhood.)

A Scrap and a Robe

by Myrina D. McCullough

PURPOSE FOR LISTENING: to enjoy and appreciate a story

READ-ALOUD TIP: Before beginning the story, review the West African words and their meanings.

A *harmattan* is a dry, dusty breeze. *Damask* is a patterned fabric.

The West African Harmattan (HAR-mah-tan) whipped up a billow of dust. Suddenly Sali spied a scrap of glorious orange damask cloth turning in the hot wind like a flame. She followed as it danced down a street she didn't know very well. She skipped over holes and skirted people on chairs.

All at once the wind died down, and the scrap settled gently on the scratchy, sandy road.

Sali picked up the cloth and gazed at it with admiring eyes. She turned it this way and that in the sun and imagined herself in a flowing dlokibani (dloak-ee-bah-NEE) made of such cloth.

A *dlokibani* is a special holiday robe.

This was a treasure, and she would take it home for her little wooden doll. It would surely make a lovely headpiece for that lucky one.

Sali wandered back the way she had come, slowly now. At the corner of the street, she passed the table vendor, who was selling his dusty packets of tea and two-pill packs of aspirin. She passed Ami's mother, roasting peanuts and selling them by the handful. She turned onto the larger street and passed a plastic-goods store that displayed rows and rows of brightly colored plastic plates, bowls, and teapots. She glanced into the next shop and then stopped short. It was a fabric shop! There on the high counter was an entire bolt of the same wondrous cloth she held in her hand!

She felt afraid at first, as though the little scrap she had found did not belong to her. She moved quickly on. When she got home, Sali put the orange swatch into her trunk, next to her wooden doll.

The next day Sali went back to the cloth shop. She stood near the door and watched the storekeeper. He measured and cut, as one person after another bought pieces of cloth. Her prized orange damask was back on a high shelf to the rear of the store.

After a while the shopkeeper looked at Sali. "Why do you stand so long at the door?" he asked.

What do you think Sali will say to the shopkeeper?

Sali took a deep breath and said, "I would like to help you in the store till I could earn enough of that orange cloth to make a dlokibani for myself."

The orange fabric glowed in a shaft of light from the uncovered bulb at the back of the store.

"That is very special and expensive cloth, little one," the shopkeeper told her.

"I can work a long time," replied Sali.

So she swept the courtyard and threw away scraps. She pushed big rolls of cloth back and forth. She ran to buy cough drops and peanuts and kola nuts for the shopkeeper. For days and days she worked.

Finally, one day the store owner lifted down the lustrous roll of orange damask and measured out several yards. "You've worked well for this cloth, Sali," he said. "I thank you."

Lustrous means "Shiny."

Sali rushed straight home with her treasure. Carefully she placed the cloth in her trunk.

But how was she to get the dloki made? Sali did not know how to sew. Her mother always had their clothes made by a tailor who sat in a tiny shop several blocks from their house.

Dloki is short for *dlokibani.*

Sali went and stood under a tree near the tailor's shop. She watched the people come and go. The tailor would whip out his measuring tape and see how tall the people were, how fat they were, how long their arms, how short their necks. He measured every part of them.

After almost a whole day the tailor noticed Sali.

"What are you doing there, little girl?" he asked.

"I have some beautiful cloth," she said, "and I want it sewn into a dlokibani. Could I work for you to pay for sewing it into a robe for me?"

The tailor agreed. Once again Sali worked for days and days. She swept and fanned the tea coals and held scissors and bought thread.

At last, the tailor said, "Bring me the cloth, Sali."

Sali rushed home and brought back the satiny, shining cloth. She also brought her doll, its small head still neatly wrapped in the swatch of orange.

The tailor took his tape and measured Sali, shoulder to ankle, shoulder to elbow, left shoulder to right shoulder. Then he started cutting the billows of orange fabric. Sali watched until the sun set and the sky grew dark.

> How do you think Sali will get her cloth made into a robe?

When at last she went home, her mother was watching for her. "Sali, where have you been so late in the evening!" she scolded. "What are you up to all day long? You never stay home anymore to help and learn to do things!"

"Mama," Sali said, "tomorrow I will show you where I've been and what I've learned."

The next day was an important holiday called Tabaski (tah-bas-KEE). Drums were beating in many neighborhoods. Relatives and friends came to visit Sali's family.

Sali slipped quietly away. Soon her mother missed her. "Now where has Sali gone?" she exclaimed.

Just then, Sali walked in, proudly wearing a beautiful orange dloki with a matching headdress. In her arms she carried her doll, dressed exactly as she was!

"Mama, look," Sali said. "I have learned about selling cloth and running a store. I've learned about measuring people and sewing clothes. I've learned that when I work hard, I can get what I want. Look at my beautiful dlokibani!"

---

1. **What does Sali learn?** (Possible response: She learns that if you work hard, you can get something you want.)

2. **Why do you think the author chose the title "A Scrap and a Robe"?** (Possible response: The title tells about two parts of the story—how Sali first saw the scrap of orange fabric and how she found a way to get a robe made from that fabric.)

Aurora Means Dawn

by Scott Russell Sanders

PURPOSE FOR LISTENING: to respond appropriately to questions

READ-ALOUD TIP: Display a map of the United States and point out the route from Connecticut to Ohio.

When Mr. and Mrs. Sheldon reached Ohio in 1800 with seven children, two oxen, and a bulging wagon, they were greeted by a bone-rattling thunderstorm.

The younger children wailed.

The older children spoke of returning to Connecticut.

> Have students set a purpose for listening.

The oxen pretended to be four-legged boulders and would budge neither forward nor backward, for all of Mr. Sheldon's thwacking. Lightning toppled so many oaks and elms across the wagon track that even a dozen agreeable oxen would have done them no good, in any case.

> Why won't the oxen move?

They camped. More precisely, they spent the night squatting in mud beneath the wagon, trying to keep dry.

Every few minutes, Mrs. Sheldon would count the children, touching each head in turn, to make sure none of the seven had vanished in the deluge.

> A *deluge* is a great flood or fall of rain.

Mrs. Sheldon remarked to her husband that there had never been any storms even remotely like this one back in Connecticut. "Nor any cheap land," he replied. "No land's cheap if you perish before setting eyes on it," she said. A boom of thunder ended talk.

They fell asleep to the roar of rain.

> Why are the Sheldons moving to Ohio?

Next morning, it was hard to tell just where the wagon track had been, there were so many trees down.

Husband and wife tried cutting their way forward.

After chopping up and dragging aside only a few felled trees, and with half the morning gone, they decided Mr. Sheldon should go fetch help from Aurora, their destination.

On the land-company map they had carried from the East, Aurora was advertised as a village, with mill and store and clustered cabins. But the actual place turned out to consist of a surveyor's post topped by a red streamer.

So Mr. Sheldon walked to the next village shown on the map — Hudson, which fortunately did exist, and by morning he'd found eight men who agreed to help him clear the road. Their axes flashed for hours in the sunlight. It took them until late afternoon to reach the wagon.

Who helps the
Sheldon family
reach Aurora?

With the track cleared, the oxen still could not move the wagon through the mud until all nine men and one woman and every child except the toddler and the baby put their shoulders to the wheels.

They reached Aurora at dusk, making out the surveyor's post in the lantern light. The men from Hudson insisted on returning that night to their own homes. Ax blades glinted on their shoulders as they disappeared from the circle of the campfire.

Huddled together like a basketful of kittens, the children slept in the hollow of a sycamore tree. Mr. and Mrs. Sheldon carried the lantern in circles around the sycamore, gazing at this forest that would become their farm. Aurora meant dawn; they knew that. And their family was the dawn of dawn, the first glimmering in this new place.

1. **The name of the town, Aurora, means "dawn," or the start of a new day. How does the end of the story show the start of a new life for the Sheldon family?** (Possible response: They have finally reached Aurora. They are the first family to settle there. They will build their farm on that land.)

2. **What did you learn about life in 1800 from listening to this story?** (Possible response: Traveling by wagon was a slow, difficult way to reach a new place.)

Myths and Fables

Atalanta

by Betty Miles

PURPOSE FOR LISTENING: to interpret and evaluate a myth

READ-ALOUD TIP: Have the tone of your voice reflect the excitement of the race.

Once upon a time, not long ago, there lived a princess named Atalanta, who could run as fast as the wind.

Have students set a purpose for listening.

She was so bright, and so clever, and could build things and fix things so wonderfully, that many young men wished to marry her.

"What shall I do?" said Atalanta's father, who was a powerful king. "So many young men want to marry you, and I don't know how to choose."

"You don't have to choose, Father," Atalanta said. "I will choose. And I'm not sure that I will choose to marry anyone at all."

"Of course you will," said the king. "Everybody gets married. It is what people do."

"But," Atalanta told him, with a toss of her head, "I intend to go out and see the world. When I come home, perhaps I will marry and perhaps I will not."

The king did not like this at all. He was a very ordinary king; that is, he was powerful and used to having his own way. So he did not answer Atalanta, but simply told her, "I have decided how to choose the young man you will marry. I will hold a great race, and the winner — the swiftest, fleetest young man of all — will win the right to marry you."

Now Atalanta was a clever girl as well as a swift runner. She saw that she might win both the argument and the race — provided that she herself could run in the race, too. "Very well," she said. "But you must let me race along with the others. If I am not the winner, I will accept the wishes of the young man who is."

The king agreed to this. He was pleased; he would have his way, marry off his daughter, and enjoy a fine day of racing as well. So he directed his messengers to travel throughout the kingdom announcing the race with its wonderful prize: the chance to marry the bright Atalanta.

Why does Atalanta want to run in the race?

As the day of the race drew near, flags were raised in the streets of the town, and banners were hung near the grassy field where the race would be run. Baskets of ripe plums and peaches, wheels of cheese, ropes of sausages and onions, and loaves of crusty bread were gathered for the crowds.

Meanwhile, Atalanta herself was preparing for the race. Each day at dawn, dressed in soft green trousers and a shirt of yellow silk, she went to the field in secret and ran across it — slowly at first, then fast and faster, until she could run the course more quickly than anyone had ever run it before.

What does Atalanta do to make sure she will win the race?

As the day of the race grew nearer, young men began to crowd into the town. Each was sure he could win the prize, except for one; that was Young John, who lived in the town. He saw Atalanta day by day as she bought nails and wood to make a pigeon house, or chose parts for her telescope, or laughed with her friends. Young John saw the princess only from a distance, but near enough to know how bright and clever she was. He wished very much to race with her, to win, and to earn the right to talk with her and become her friend.

"For surely," he said to himself, "it is not right for Atalanta's father to give her away to the winner of the race. Atalanta herself must choose the person she wants to marry, or whether she wishes to marry at all. Still, if I could only win the race, I would be free to speak to her, and to ask for her friendship."

Each evening, after his studies of the stars and the seas, Young John went to the field in secret and practiced running across it. Night after night, he ran fast as the wind across the twilight field, until he could cross it more quickly than anyone had ever crossed it before.

What does Young John like about Atalanta?

At last, the day of the race arrived.

Trumpets sounded in the early morning, and the young men gathered at the edge of the field, along with Atalanta herself, the prize they sought. The king and his friends sat in soft chairs, and the townspeople stood along the course.

The king rose to address them all. "Good day," he said to the crowds. "Good luck," he said to the young men. To Atalanta he said, "Good-bye. I must tell you farewell, for tomorrow you will be married."

Does the king think Atlanta will win the race? How do you know?

"I am not so sure of that, Father," Atalanta answered. She was dressed for the race in trousers of crimson and a shirt of silk as blue as the sky, and she laughed as she looked up and down the line of young men.

"Not one of them," she said to herself, "can win the race, for I will run fast as the wind and leave them all behind."

And now a bugle sounded, a flag was dropped, and the runners were off!

The crowds cheered as the young men and Atalanta began to race across the field. At first they ran as a group, but Atalanta soon pulled ahead, with three of the young men close after her. As they neared the halfway point, one young man put on a great burst of speed and seemed to pull ahead for an instant, but then he gasped and fell back. Atalanta shot on.

Soon another young man, tense with the effort, drew near to Atalanta. He reached out as though to touch her sleeve, stumbled for an instant, and lost speed. Atalanta smiled as she ran on. I have almost won, she thought.

But then another young man came near. This was Young John, running like the wind, as steadily and as swiftly as Atalanta herself. Atalanta felt his closeness, and in a sudden burst she dashed ahead.

> Who do you think will win the race?

Young John might have given up at this, but he never stopped running. Nothing at all, thought he, will keep me from winning the chance to speak with Atalanta. And on he ran, swift as the wind, until he ran as her equal, side by side

Young John ran as her equal means that he and Atalanta were running at the same speed and with the same skill.

with her, toward the golden ribbon that marked the race's end. Atalanta raced even faster to pull ahead, but Young John was a strong match for her. Smiling with the pleasure of the race, Atalanta and Young John reached the finish line together, and together they broke through the golden ribbon.

Trumpets blew. The crowd shouted and leaped about. The king rose. "Who is that young man?" he asked.

"It is Young John from the town," the people told him.

"Very well. Young John," said the king, as John and Atalanta stood before him, exhausted and jubilant from their efforts. "You have not won the race, but you have come closer to winning than any man here. And so I give you the prize that was promised—the right to marry my daughter."

What do you think Young John will say?

Young John smiled at Atalanta, and she smiled back. "Thank you, sir," said John to the king, "but I could not possibly marry your daughter unless she wished to marry me. I have run this race for the chance to talk with Atalanta, and, if she is willing, I am ready to claim my prize."

Atalanta laughed with pleasure. "And I," she said to John, "could not possibly marry before I have seen the world. But I would like nothing better than to spend the afternoon with you."

Then the two of them sat and talked on the grassy field, as the crowds went away. They ate bread and cheese and purple plums. Atalanta told John about her telescopes and her pigeons, and John told Atalanta about his globes and his studies of geography. At the end of the day, they were friends.

On the next day, John sailed off to discover new lands. And Atalanta set off to visit the great cities.

By this time, each of them has had wonderful adventures, and seen marvelous sights. Perhaps some day they will be married, and perhaps they will not. In any case, they are friends. And it is certain that they are both living happily ever after.

> What do you think Atalanta will say? Do they ever get married?

---

1. **What prize does Young John want to win?** (Possible response: He wants a chance to talk to Atalanta.)

2. **Do you think Young John and Atalanta make the right choices? Why or why not?** (Responses will vary.)

The Country Mouse and the City Mouse

an Aesop fable

PURPOSE FOR LISTENING: to listen responsively to a fable

READ-ALOUD TIP: Read this fable slowly so that children have time to absorb the complex language and sentence structure.

Have students set a purpose for listening.

An honest, plain, sensible Country Mouse invited her city friend for a visit. When the City Mouse arrived, the Country Mouse opened her heart and hearth in honor of her old friend. There was not a morsel that she did not bring forth out of her larder — peas and barley, cheese parings and nuts — hoping by quantity to make up for what she feared was wanting in quality, eating nothing herself, lest her guest

should not have enough. The City Mouse, condescending to pick a bit here and a bit there, at length exclaimed, "My dear, please let me speak freely to you. How can you endure the dullness of your life here, with nothing but woods and meadows, mountains and brooks about? You can't really prefer these empty fields to streets teeming with carriages and men! Do you not long for the conversation of the world instead of the chirping of birds? I promise you will find the city a change for the better. Let's away this moment!"

Overpowered with such fine words and so polished a manner, the Country Mouse agreed, and they set out on their journey. About midnight they entered a great house, where the City Mouse lived. Here were couches of crimson velvet, ivory

Why does the Country Mouse decide to visit the city?

carvings, and on the table were the remains of a splendid banquet. The Country Mouse was placed in the midst of a rich Persian carpet, and it was now the turn of the City Mouse to play hostess. She ran to and fro to supply all her guest's wants, serving dish upon dish and dainty upon dainty. The Country Mouse sat and enjoyed herself, delighted with this new turn of affairs. Just as she was thinking with contempt of the poor life she had forsaken, the door flew open and a noisy party burst into the room. The frightened friends scurried for the first corner they could find. No sooner did they peek out than the barking of dogs drove them back in greater terror

What do you think the Country Mouse will do?

than before. At length, when things seemed quiet, the Country Mouse stole from her hiding place and bade her friend good-bye, whispering, "Oh, my dear, this fine mode of living may do for you, but I prefer my poor barley in peace and quiet to dining at the richest feast where Fear and Danger lie waiting."

A simple life in peace and safety is preferable to a life of luxury spent in fear.

1. **Would you choose the life of the Country Mouse or the City Mouse?** (Responses will vary.)

2. **Tell the lesson of "The Country Mouse and the City Mouse" in your own words.** (Possible response: It's better to live with less in a safe place than to have fine things in a place where you have to worry all the time.)

THE CLEVER WARTHOG

an African fable retold by George Schaller

PURPOSE FOR LISTENING: to enjoy and appreciate a fable

READ-ALOUD TIP: As you read this African fable, imitate the plaintive tone of the warthog's voice.

Once upon a time a warthog took shelter in a cave.

A lion suddenly entered the cave. The warthog immediately pretended to support the roof of the cave with its tusks and called plaintively: "Lion, lion, help me hold up the roof for it is falling and we shall both be killed."

Why does the warthog ask the lion to help him hold up the roof of the cave?

Thereupon the lion held up the roof with his paws. The warthog then said to him: "You are much stronger than I. Just hold up the roof while I fetch some logs to prop it up." The vain lion was flattered and agreed to stay. And the warthog escaped.

1. **Fables are often used to teach a lesson. What lesson did you learn from this fable?** (Responses will vary.)

2. **Why does the lion stay in the cave after the warthog leaves?** (Possible responses: The lion wants to show the warthog that he is strong. The lion thinks the roof will fall on him if he doesn't hold it up.)

Folktales

Fish, Flowers, and Fruit

by Joyce Sidman

PURPOSE FOR LISTENING: to connect ideas with those of others

READ-ALOUD TIP: Display a map of the world, and point out the island of Palau, the westernmost of the Caroline Islands in the western Pacific.

Long ago, in the village of Ngiwal (NGEE-wahl) on the island of Palau (puh-LOW) in the waters of the great Pacific Ocean, lived a girl named Mora. Life was hard in Ngiwal. The soil was bad and wouldn't grow taro, so the villagers had to spend each day

> *Taro* is a tropical plant that has starchy, edible roots.

trapping and netting and spearing fish. Mora worked alongside the others, but when she had a free moment, she liked to go off exploring.

One day she swam out to a small reef island where no one lived. At the center of its tangled jungle, Mora discovered a most unusual tree. This tree had leaves as green as the ocean and as shiny as the sun, and it was covered all over with round, prickly flowers.

The flowers were so odd that Mora reached out and picked one. To her astonishment, a tiny fish hopped out from the broken stem and wriggled in her hand! She picked another flower. Another tiny fish came wriggling out. Mora looked up at the tall, many-flowered tree and thought of her village, which often had to go without food.

> Do you think Mora will tell others about the tree? Why?

"If there is a fish in each of these flowers," she said to herself, "this tree could feed us all!" She tucked the flower and the fish in the band of her skirt and swam back to Ngiwal as fast as she could.

First she went to her mother and told her about the tree. Her mother shook her head. "Such foolishness," she said.

Then she went to her father. "A happy dream," he sighed.

So she went to find the elder in his wooden bai. She

A *bai* is a special house where ceremonies are held.

spoke respectfully: "On the small reef island by the village of Ngiwal on the island of Palau in the wide waters of the Pacific, there is a tree with fish in its flowers."

The elder looked her up and down. "An amazing story, Granddaughter! How do I know it is true?"

From her skirt, Mora drew out the strange flower and the tiny fish and placed them in his hand.

"Show me this tree," the elder said. He gathered four villagers, and they paddled to the island in a canoe.

Mora led them to the tree. Sure enough, when the elder stepped up and plucked a flower, a fish came out from the broken stem.

The others gasped, "What wonders!" Soon they were all plucking the odd, prickly flowers and catching the tiny fish that jumped out.

"Still, it is only a handful of minnows," said one of the villagers, drawing back an ax. "Let us cut a branch and see

what happens." He swung and hacked off a thick limb. Out flopped a big, silvery tuna.

"We will never have to fish again!" the villagers cheered.

The tree on the small reef island near the village of Ngiwal on the island of Palau in the waters of the great Pacific Ocean provided many fish for the villagers. All they needed to do was lop off a branch, and out flowed enough fish to feed them. They grew fat and happy, and the memory of their hardship faded.

What do you think will happen to the tree?

One day when Mora swam out to visit the tree, she noticed that it was no longer as green as the ocean nor as shiny as the sun. Most of its leaves were gone, and there were few branches left. Worse yet, when the villagers' axes bit into the tree, she heard the sound of weeping.

"The spirit of the tree is unhappy," she said to the villagers gathering fish. "I hear it crying in pain."

"We hear nothing," the villagers said. "Besides, if the tree's spirit were unhappy, why would it continue to give us fish?"

Mora had no answer. But as they paddled away, an old woman appeared beneath the tree. Tears ran down her wrinkled cheeks, and she held out an empty bowl.

"Why are you weeping, Grandmother?" Mora asked.

The old woman looked up. "Ah!" she said sadly. "I weep because my bowl is empty."

"But here is the tree that gives us fish," Mora said.

"This tree is dying," the old woman wept. "Soon, the sharp blades of the axes will kill it, and I will have nothing left to eat."

"What shall we do?" Mora asked. "Surely this wondrous tree was meant to feed us."

The woman looked at her with eyes like an old turtle's. "The flower that is picked cannot bear fruit." With that, she disappeared.

Mora sat for a long time beneath the tree, thinking about what the old woman had said. She leaned against its rough bark and stared up at the few green limbs that grew strong and straight. She parted the petals of a flower and found a tiny pip of fruit. "The flower that is picked cannot bear fruit," she murmured to herself. And she knew what she had to do.

The next morning, when the villagers came with their axes, they found Mora beneath the tree. "Step back, Daughter. We are here to gather the day's fish."

"Not today," Mora said firmly. "The tree is ill. It needs a day to heal. Ask the elder; he will believe me."

The villagers stared at her suspiciously. She was just a young girl, but the elder had once listened to her. Reluctantly, they went away, vowing to be back the next day.

When they returned, Mora stood in their way again. "The tree is not yet healed," she said. "Tell the elder one more day is necessary."

"This is foolishness!" the villagers grumbled as they stomped away. But Mora just smiled, for the prickly flowers were losing their petals.

What do you think Mora will do?

What is Mora waiting for?

On the third day, the villagers brought the elder with them.

"Daughter, the village is hungry," he said. "We must gather fish from the tree."

How does Mora protect the tree?

"What about our spears and fishing nets, Grandfather?" Mora asked respectfully. "Have we forgotten how to use them?"

The elder frowned, and the villagers muttered. In truth, they *had* begun to forget how to fish the old ways.

"We are hungry!" someone called. "Stand aside!" The rest raised their axes.

What do you think Mora will do? Why do you think this?

"But look at the tree!" Mora pointed upward. All the strange, prickly flowers had disappeared, and in their place were wrinkled green globes the size of fists. Swiftly, Mora climbed up and shook a branch. One of the globes dropped and split in half, revealing a white, fleshy core.

"What is this fruit?" the elder cried, snatching it up. "We have never seen its like before. Cooks!" he ordered. "Hurry back to the village and see what can be made of this!"

Much could be made of the strange fruit, they soon discovered. It could be baked, fried, and pickled, and it filled the stomach wonderfully. The elder gave it a name, breadfruit, and declared that, from then on, no ax should touch the tree from whence it came.

The breadfruit tree grew once again as green as the ocean and as glossy as the sun. Mora took to carrying its seeds with her, planting them wherever she went. Soon there were enough trees to feed the whole village of Ngiwal — and indeed the entire island of Palau.

> Do you think the villagers will cut the branches from the tree again? Why or why not?

When the villagers yearned for fish, they took up their spears and nets and went out on the wide waters of the Pacific. They remembered the old ways of fishing and passed them on to their sons and daughters. They passed on, too, the story of Mora, the girl who stopped the axes of Ngiwal and turned the flowers of fish into fruit.

1. **What are Mora's special qualities? Do you think she could save the tree if she were not like this?** (Possible response: Mora is caring and courageous. Responses to the second question will vary.)

2. **What do the villagers pass on to their children?** (Possible response: They pass on the old ways of fishing as well as the story of Mora, the girl who turned the flowers of fish into fruit.)

The Bat

a Central Asian tale
retold by Pleasant DeSpain

PURPOSE FOR LISTENING: **to enjoy and appreciate a folktale**

READ-ALOUD TIP: Use distinctive voices for each of the three animals in this folktale.

Once long ago, the bat did not sleep during the day and fly only at night as he does now. Instead he was wide awake during the daylight hours and he flew about the sky with all the birds.

> Have children set a purpose for listening.

One bright and sunny day he met an eagle winging his way across the sky.

"Friend Bat," called the eagle, "I have been searching everywhere for you."

"And what is it you want from me?" asked the bat.

"Your fair share of the taxes. All the other birds have paid theirs."

"I am not of the bird family," explained the bat. "Why should I pay if I am not a bird?"

"But you have wings and you fly like a bird," said the eagle. "We are flying together right now. Thus it is only fair that you pay too."

"Watch, friend Eagle, and I will prove to you that I am not a bird." And so saying, the bat flew to the ground and ran into the woods on four feet.

"He was right!" exclaimed the eagle. "He is not a bird. He is an animal!"

> How does the bat prove to the eagle that he is not a bird?

The bat soon came to a shady brook, and because he was tired from all of his running, stopped to rest.

Soon a thirsty tiger came to the stream to drink, and seeing the bat, said, "How glad I am to meet you at last, friend Bat. I've been looking for you for several months."

"For what reason?" asked the bat.

"Oh, a very important reason, I assure you," explained the tiger. "It seems that all the animals in the forest have paid their taxes. That is, all but you."

"I am not of the animal family," said the bat. "Why should I pay if I am not an animal?"

"But you walk on four feet just like all the other animals," replied the tiger, "so you must pay your share. It is only fair."

"Watch, friend Tiger, and I will prove to you that I am not an animal."

And so saying, the bat unfolded his wings and flew high into the air.

"It is true!" exclaimed the tiger. "The bat is not an animal after all. He is a bird!"

The bat didn't want to meet the tiger ever again, so he stopped using his small legs for walking, and soon they withered away. Nor did he fly during the daylight hours, since he didn't want to meet the eagle. Thus it is that he sleeps in dark caves by day and flies only at night, when the eagle rests.

> What do you think the bat will do next?

1. **How does the bat avoid meeting both the tiger and the eagle?** (Possible response: The bat stops using his legs for walking and does not fly during the day.)

2. **Do you think the bat's actions are clever? Why or why not?** (Responses will vary.)

The Theft of a Smell

a Peruvian tale
retold by Pleasant DeSpain

PURPOSE FOR LISTENING: to listen responsively

READ-ALOUD TIP: Pause before the last paragraph and then read the judge's decision in a serious tone of voice.

Once upon a time, there lived a stingy baker in the city of Lima, Peru. Early each morning he mixed flour, milk, eggs, and raisins and baked his bread, rolls, and cookies. Then he placed the delicious goods in the open window of his shop and sold them to his customers.

The baker was so stingy that he never gave so much as a crumb of his baked goods away, even if it was a stale crumb and the birds were hungry.

The baker's neighbor, however, was a much different kind of man. He enjoyed a leisurely life and never cared about money or a steady job. In fact, one of his greatest pleasures was smelling the wonderful aromas of the baked goods in the baker's open window. The cool breeze carried the luscious smells to him like a gift each morning. He especially liked the odor of fresh-baked cinnamon rolls.

> How are the baker and his neighbor different?

The selfish baker knew that his neighbor was benefiting from his hard work and he felt that the lazy fellow shouldn't be allowed to have such enjoyment for free. Thus the baker went to his neighbor and said, "You may no longer steal the smell of my baked goods from me. You must pay me ten gold pieces each month for such a privilege. If not, I'll take you to court."

The neighbor laughed and said that it was a good joke! Then he told all the other neighbors about the baker's special smelling fee, and soon the baker was the laughingstock of the city. This made him angry enough to speak to a judge.

> A *laughingstock* is a person that others make fun of. Why does the baker become a laughingstock?

The judge had a good sense of humor, and after hearing the complaint, ordered both the baker and the neighbor to

appear before him the following day. He also ordered the neighbor to bring ten pieces of gold. The baker was quite pleased to hear this and could already feel the weight of the gold in his pocket.

The next day the courtroom was packed with curious citizens. The judge entered and asked the baker and his neighbor to approach the bench and tell their stories. The baker spoke at length about the beautiful aromas produced by his delicious pastries and how his neighbor had enjoyed them each morning for several years without ever paying so much as a penny for them.

The judge listened patiently to all the baker had to say and then asked the neighbor if he had in fact enjoyed the smells without paying for them. The neighbor replied, "Yes, your honor, it is true."

The judge again spoke to the neighbor, "Take the ten gold pieces from your pocket and shake them in your hand so that we can hear them clink together."

The man was surprised at such a strange request but did as he was told.

"Did you hear the clinking of your neighbor's gold coins?" the judge asked the baker.

"Yes, your honor," said the baker.

"And does the sound of gold coins clinking together please your ears?"

"Yes," replied the baker.

> Why do you think the judge wants the neighbor to shake the gold coins?

"This, then, is my decision," said the judge. "The neighbor has enjoyed the smell of baked goods. In return, the baker has enjoyed the sound of gold coins. Case dismissed!"

> What do you think will be the judge's decision?

---

1. **Do you think the judge's decision is fair? Explain.**
   (Responses will vary.)

2. **Do you think the baker will be happy with the judge's decision?** (Possible response: The baker will be angry because he wants his neighbor to pay him for smelling the baked goods. But because he has lost his case, he won't get any money.)

The Three Little Pigs

a folktale from England
retold by Jane Yolen

PURPOSE FOR LISTENING: to listen responsively

READ-ALOUD TIP: Use different voices for the wolf and the three little pigs. The third pig should sound more mature than the other two.

Once upon a time there was an old sow who had three little pigs. She loved those little pigs and kept them warm and fed. But they grew and grew, and she was so poor she could no longer keep them, so she sent them out into the world to seek their fortunes.

> Have students set a purpose for listening.

But before they left, she gave them each a clean hankie and a word of warning. "Look out," she said, "for the wolf at your door." Then, with her own hankie, she waved good-bye.

And they went trotting off down the road.

Now, the first little pig met a man with a bundle of straw. "Please, man," said the little pig, "give me that straw to make a house. I will give you my hankie in exchange." And as it was a beautiful hankie, the man did. The little pig stitched and sewed and patted and pushed the straw into shape, and soon he had a fine straw house.

"I like my straw house," said the little pig, and he went in and closed the door behind.

But pretty soon along came a wolf, and he knocked at the door. "Little pig, little pig, let me come in."

The little pig looked out of the straw window and saw the wolf and remembered what his mama had told him. "Not by the hair of my chinny-chin-chin."

Why won't the little pig let the wolf inside his new house?

The wolf's face got red and his ears stuck straight out. He drew himself up, tall as a tree. "Then," he said, "I'll huff. And I'll puff. And I'll blow your house down."

Then he huffed and he puffed and he blew the house down.

The little pig ran out the back door all the way to his brother's house.

Now, the second little pig had met a man with a bundle of sticks. "Please, man," said the little pig, "give me those sticks to make a house. I will give you my hankie in exchange." And as it was a beautiful hankie, the man did. The little pig hammered and sawed and shoved and shifted those sticks into shape, and soon he had a fine stick house.

"I like my stick house," said the little pig, and he went in and closed the door behind.

Just then there was a *rat-a-tat-tat* on the door, and when he opened it, there was his brother, sweaty and out of breath. He let his brother in.

"The wolf — " the first little pig had barely gotten out when the wolf was at the door.

"Little pig, little pig," said the wolf, "let me come in."

The little pig, remembering what his mama had said and seeing the state his brother was in, replied, "Not by the hair of my chinny-chin-chin."

Sticks are stronger than straw. Do you think the wolf can blow down a house made of sticks?

Do you think the wolf will blow down the house made of bricks? Why or why not?

The wolf's nose began to drip and the hairs on his tail got quite stiff. He drew himself up, tall as a tree. "Then," he said, "I'll huff. And I'll puff. And I'll blow your house down."

Then he huffed and he puffed and he blew the house down.

Both little pigs ran out the back door all the way to their brother's house.

Now, the third little pig had met a man with a load of bricks. "Please, man," said the little pig, "give me those bricks to build a house with and I will work for you this week." The man gave him the bricks and showed him the best way to build a house, and the little pig stacked and styled and laid those bricks the proper way, and eventually he had a fine brick house.

Pretty soon his brothers showed up, dazed and scared, and he let them in.

"The wolf — " they both gasped. So he gave them each some hot chocolate and put them to bed. And no sooner had he settled in his chair when there was a hard and hearty knock at the door.

"Little pig, little pig," called the wolf, "let me come in."

The little pig shook his head. "Not by the hair of my chinny-chin-chin."

The wolf's eyes grew squinty and his teeth ground together. He drew himself up, tall as a tree. "Then," he said, "I'll huff. And I'll puff. And I'll blow your house down."

Well, he huffed.

And he puffed.

And he huffed.

And he puffed.

And he huffedandpuffedandhuffedandpuffed but he could not blow the house down. So he growled and yowled and moaned and groaned and decided then and there that he would climb down the chimney and get that little pig.

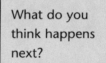

When the little pig heard wolf claws on his window, he wondered. When he heard wolf claws on his walls, he worried. But when he heard wolf claws going across his roof and over to his chimney, he knew just what to do. Still hanging over the blazing fire was the pot of water he had used to make his brothers' hot chocolate. So when he heard the wolf start down the chimney, he took the cover off the pot.

What do you think happens next?

The wolf came down — *splat* — right in the bubbling water, and it boiled the hair right off him. He screamed and howled and ran out the door. Then he moved way to the south, where he could be warm without his fur coat, and never bothered the pigs again.

And as for the three little pigs, they built a brick cottage next door for their mama, and they all lived happily ever after.

1. **Have you heard this story before? How is this telling like and different from those you have heard before?**
(Responses will vary.)

2. **What lesson do the three little pigs learn?** (Possible response: They learn it is worth the extra work to build a strong house.)

Why Birds Are Never Hungry

a Hmong folk story
by Norma J. Livo and Dia Cha

PURPOSE FOR LISTENING: to interpret and evaluate a folktale

READ-ALOUD TIP: While reading this folktale, pause before the last paragraph to emphasize why birds are never hungry.

A long time ago, when the world was new, there were two brothers who went hunting, After the long day of walking through the jungle, they got lost. They were worried and could not remember which way to go to get back home to their parents. For many days, they wandered in the jungle. They did not have anything to eat and became very hungry.

Have students set a purpose for listening.

One day the older brother decided that he had to go to find food and wood for the fire. The younger brother also wanted to go to gather water. After they discussed their plans, they each went their own way. They agreed to meet back at the clearing in the forest where they were camping when they had gathered the necessary things.

The younger brother went up and down everywhere through the jungle, but he could not find any water. Finally, he was so tired he sat down on a stone to think. He tried to face in a different direction, thinking he might find water that way. While he was thinking, a bluebird was jumping from one tree to another, singing, "I know where your parents are, I know where your parents are!"

Why is the younger brother determined to hear what the bluebird is singing?

The younger brother was surprised, because he wasn't sure what he was really hearing. He stared at the bluebird and tried to listen more carefully. He hoped the bluebird would sing to him and say those words again. He watched

the bluebird wherever it went. After a time the bluebird started to sing again, saying the same words. The younger brother asked the bluebird, "Did you say you know where our parents are?"

"Yes, I did. But this is a bargain. If you can give me three insects then I will lead you to your parents," the bluebird chirped.

The boy paused a while and then he said, "Are you sure? If you are sure, will you also follow me now while I go to get my older brother?"

The bird agreed.

As the bargain had been set, the bluebird followed the younger boy to the clearing in the forest, where the older brother was sitting and waiting. He had been there for a long time and had returned without either the food or the wood. The younger brother told the older brother about his bargain with the bluebird. Then the brothers left the bird in the clearing and went to find the insects. It took them quite some time, but they finally returned to the clearing and gave the insects to the bluebird.

> After they meet the bluebird, what do the brothers look for in the forest? Do they find what they are looking for?

After the bluebird had eaten the insects he said, "You boys must follow me wherever I fly and I will lead you to your parents."

The bluebird flew away, leading the two boys. They followed the bird closely, and after many days they finally got home. They were very happy, and they thanked the bluebird many times for leading them safely home.

Before the bluebird left the two brothers to go back to the forest, the boys told him, "We will never forget how you helped us. We hope that we can help you one day — to save your life, too. We will always give you food when you are hungry."

And that is why birds are always around people's houses now — because of the promise given to the bluebird by the two grateful brothers.

1. **What is the bargain between the bluebird and the boy? Do you think it is fair?** (Possible response: If the boy gives the bluebird three insects, the bird will show the boy how to find his parents. Responses to the second question will vary.)

2. **What do the two brothers do to thank the bird?** (Possible response: To thank the bird, the brothers always give him food when he is hungry.)

How the Girl Taught the Coyotes to Sing Harmony

a story from the Southwest
by Nancy Wood

PURPOSE FOR LISTENING: to enjoy and appreciate a folktale

READ-ALOUD TIP: Play a recording of coyotes howling to add another dimension to this folktale.

When coyotes first came into the world, they were bad singers. One sang high, another sang low. Another sang off-key. Too loud. Too soft. Too shrill. The other animals, who couldn't sing at all, called those coyotes a bunch of screech owls. "We're not screech owls," the coyotes said. "We're coyotes."

"Prove it," the other animals said, certain the coyotes would fail.

Have students set a purpose for listening.

So the coyotes started out across the land to find a way to sing better.

They sang on top of mountains. They sang in the middle of the desert. They sang in canyons. They were still bad singers. And the other animals were still making fun of them. What could they do? They talked among themselves, but none of them had an idea.

Why do the coyotes want to find a way to sing better?

One day, as they were crossing an arroyo, they saw a girl playing her flute. The music sounded so appealing that they started to sing, very slowly and hesitantly at first. That flute could make coyote music! The girl noticed that the coyotes were singing along with it, even if they were off-key.

"Would you like me to teach you to sing harmony?" she asked.

Harmony is a combination of musical notes that sounds pleasing.

The coyotes thought about it, then decided they had to learn. After all, they couldn't stand to have the other animals laughing at them. It was very hard work at first, but those coyotes tried to sound the way the flute did, not too sweet, not too sour, not too high, and not too low. They even tried to sing all together, on the same note and pitch. Night and day they sang. Through rain and snow they sang. Summer and winter they sang. Finally, they succeeded. When they did, the other animals stopped to listen. They were amazed at how beautiful the music was.

"Imagine that," they said, trying to sound like coyotes themselves, all those badgers, deer, bear, elk, and ground squirrels who can't sing at all. They began to respect the coyotes.

Now it's the coyotes who make the nighttime sweeter with their songs. Of course, the girl helps them stay in tune. The last time anyone looked, the girl and the coyotes were out in the middle of nowhere, practicing all night long.

1. **Some folktales explain how things came to be. What does this folktale explain?** (Possible response: It explains how coyotes came to be able to sing harmony.)

2. **Why did the other animals begin to respect the coyotes?** (Possible response: The other animals were surprised at how beautiful the music of the coyotes was. They themselves couldn't sing at all.)

Half-Chicken

retold by Alma Flor Ada

Have you ever seen a weather vane? Do you know why there is a little rooster on one end, spinning around to let us know which way the wind is blowing?

> Have you ever seen a weather vane like this? Where did you see it?

Well, I'll tell you. It's an old, old story that my grandmother once told me. And before that, her grandmother told it to her. It goes like this . . .

A long, long time ago, on a Mexican ranch, a mother hen was sitting on her eggs. One by one, the baby chicks began to hatch, leaving their empty shells behind. One, two, three, four . . . twelve chicks had hatched. But the last egg still had not cracked open.

The hen did not know what to do. The chicks were running here and there, and she could not chase after them because she was still sitting on the last egg.

Finally there was a tiny sound. The baby chick was pecking at its egg from the inside. The hen quickly helped it break open the shell, and at last the thirteenth chick came out into the world.

This was no ordinary chick. He had only one wing, only one leg, only one eye, and only half as many feathers as the other chicks.

It was not long before everyone at the ranch knew that a very special chick had been born.

The ducks told the turkeys. The turkeys told the pigeons. The pigeons told the swallows. And the swallows flew over the fields, spreading the news to the cows grazing peacefully with their calves, the fierce bulls, and the swift horses.

Soon the hen was surrounded by animals who wanted to see the strange chick.

One of the ducks said, "But he only has one wing!"

And one of the turkeys added, "Why, he's only a . . . half chicken!"

From then on, everyone called him Half-Chicken. And Half-Chicken, finding himself at the center of all this attention, became very vain.

Vain means "too proud of yourself."

One day he overheard the swallows, who traveled a great deal, talking about him: "Not even at the court of the viceroy in Mexico City is there anyone so unique."

Then Half-Chicken decided that it was time for him to leave the ranch. Early one morning he said his farewells, announcing:

"Good-bye, good-bye!

I'm off to Mexico City

to see the court of the viceroy!"

And *hip hop hip hop*, off he went, hippety-hopping along on his only foot.

> A *viceroy* is someone who rules a country for his king.

Half-Chicken had not walked very far when he found a stream whose waters were blocked by some branches.

"Good morning, Half-Chicken. Would you please move the branches that are blocking my way?" asked the stream.

Half-Chicken moved the branches aside. But when the stream suggested that he stay awhile and take a swim, he answered:

"I have no time to lose.

I'm off to Mexico City

to see the court of the viceroy!"

And *hip hop hip hop,* off he went, hippety-hopping along on his only foot.

A little while later, Half-Chicken found a small fire burning between some rocks. The fire was almost out.

"Good morning, Half-Chicken. Please, fan me a little with your wing, for I am about to go out," asked the fire.

Half-Chicken fanned the fire with his wing, and it blazed up again. But when the fire suggested that he stay awhile and warm up, he answered:

"I have no time to lose.

I'm off to Mexico City

to see the court of the viceroy!"

And *hip hop hip hop*, off he went, hippety-hopping along on his only foot.

After he had walked a little farther, Half-Chicken found the wind tangled in some bushes.

"Good morning, Half-Chicken. Would you please untangle me so that I can go on my way?" asked the wind.

> What will Half-Chicken do next?

Half-Chicken untangled the branches. But when the wind suggested that he stay and play, and offered to help him fly here and there like a dry leaf, he answered:

"I have no time to lose.

I'm off to Mexico City

to see the court of the viceroy!"

And *hip hop hip hop,* off he went, hippety-hopping along on his only foot. At last he reached Mexico City.

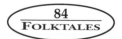

Half-Chicken crossed the enormous Great Plaza. He passed the stalls laden with meat, fish, vegetables, fruit, cheese, and honey. He passed the Parián (PAR-ee-uhn), the market where all kinds of beautiful goods were sold. Finally, he reached the gate of the viceroy's palace.

"Good afternoon," said Half-Chicken to the guards in fancy uniforms who stood in front of the palace. "I've come to see the viceroy."

One of the guards began to laugh. The other one said, "You'd better go in around the back and through the kitchen."

> Why do you think the guard sends Half-Chicken to the kitchen?

So Half-Chicken went, *hip hop hip hop,* around the palace and to the kitchen door.

The cook who saw him said, "What luck! This chicken is just what I need to make a soup for the vicereine." And he threw Half-Chicken into a kettle of water that was sitting on the fire.

When Half-Chicken felt how hot the water was, he said, "Oh, fire, help me! Please, don't burn me!"

What do you think the fire will do? How do you know?

The fire answered, "You helped me when I needed help. Now it's my turn to help you. Ask the water to jump on me and put me out."

Then Half-Chicken asked the water, "Oh, water, help me! Please jump on the fire and put it out so it won't burn me."

And the water answered, "You helped me when I needed help. Now it's my turn to help you." And it jumped on the fire and put it out.

When the cook returned, he saw that the water had spilled and the fire was out.

"This chicken has been more trouble than he's worth!" exclaimed the cook. "Besides, one of the ladies-in-waiting just told me that the vicereine doesn't want any soup. She wants to eat nothing but salad."

And he picked Half-Chicken up by his only leg and flung him out the window.

When Half-Chicken was tumbling through the air, he called out: "Oh, wind, help me, please!"

And the wind answered, "You helped me when I needed help. Now it's my turn to help you."

And the wind blew fiercely. It lifted Half-Chicken higher and higher, until the little rooster landed on one of the towers of the palace.

"From there you can see everything you want, Half-Chicken, with no danger of ending up in the cooking pot."

And from that day on, weathercocks have stood on their only leg, seeing everything that happens below and pointing whichever way their friend the wind blows.

---

1. **Who saves Half-Chicken from the cooking pot? Why?**
   (Possible response: Fire, water, and wind save Half-Chicken because he had helped each one of them.)

2. **Folktales are often stories with messages about how people should live their lives. What do you think is the message of this folktale?** (Possible response: When we act with kindness toward others, they will treat us the same way.)

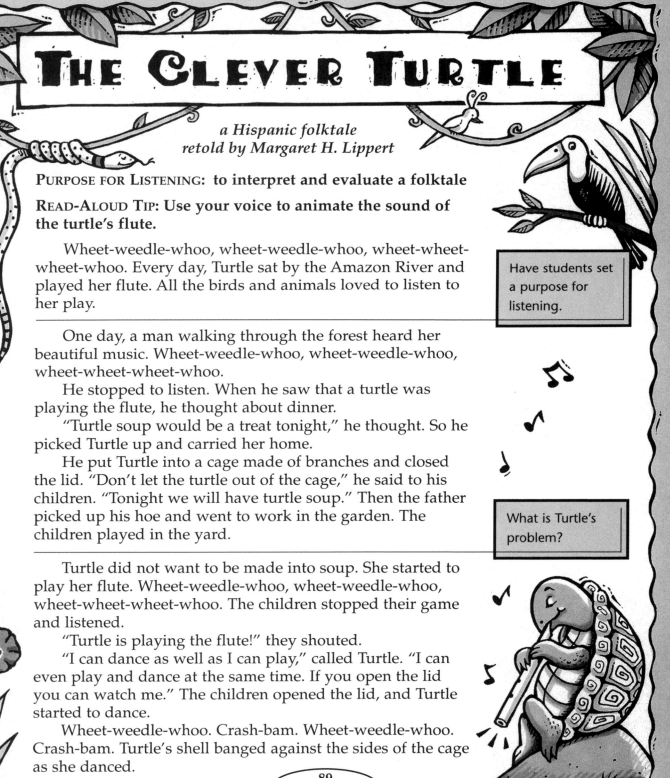

The Clever Turtle

*a Hispanic folktale
retold by Margaret H. Lippert*

PURPOSE FOR LISTENING: **to interpret and evaluate a folktale**

**READ-ALOUD TIP: Use your voice to animate the sound of
the turtle's flute.**

Wheet-weedle-whoo, wheet-weedle-whoo, wheet-wheet-
wheet-whoo. Every day, Turtle sat by the Amazon River and
played her flute. All the birds and animals loved to listen to
her play.

Have students set
a purpose for
listening.

One day, a man walking through the forest heard her
beautiful music. Wheet-weedle-whoo, wheet-weedle-whoo,
wheet-wheet-wheet-whoo.

He stopped to listen. When he saw that a turtle was
playing the flute, he thought about dinner.

"Turtle soup would be a treat tonight," he thought. So he
picked Turtle up and carried her home.

He put Turtle into a cage made of branches and closed
the lid. "Don't let the turtle out of the cage," he said to his
children. "Tonight we will have turtle soup." Then the father
picked up his hoe and went to work in the garden. The
children played in the yard.

What is Turtle's
problem?

Turtle did not want to be made into soup. She started to
play her flute. Wheet-weedle-whoo, wheet-weedle-whoo,
wheet-wheet-wheet-whoo. The children stopped their game
and listened.

"Turtle is playing the flute!" they shouted.

"I can dance as well as I can play," called Turtle. "I can
even play and dance at the same time. If you open the lid
you can watch me." The children opened the lid, and Turtle
started to dance.

Wheet-weedle-whoo. Crash-bam. Wheet-weedle-whoo.
Crash-bam. Turtle's shell banged against the sides of the cage
as she danced.

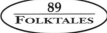

Do you think Turtle will escape? Why or why not?

The children laughed and clapped.

Turtle danced for a while, then she stopped. "I am stiff from dancing in this little cage," she said. "I need to stretch my legs. Let me go for a short walk. Then I will dance some more for you."

The children wanted to see Turtle dance again. They lifted Turtle out of the cage. "Don't go far," they said. Turtle walked around and around the yard. She walked closer and closer to the forest. Then she crawled under some leaves and disappeared.

The children looked and looked for Turtle. "Turtle! Turtle!" they called. But there was no answer. "Father will be angry," they said. "What can we do now?"

The children found a big smooth stone and painted it to look like a turtle. Then they put the painted stone in Turtle's cage. "It is dark in the cage," they said. "Father will think that the turtle is still in there."

When the father came home, he lit a fire and put some water in a pot. "Bring me the turtle," he said. The children brought the painted stone and threw it into the pot. CRASH! "The shell is hard," said the father. "But the meat will be soft when it is cooked."

After some time, the father decided the soup must be ready. He spooned the painted stone out of the pot. The stone fell onto his dish and broke it.

The father looked at the silent children. "You let the turtle go," he said. "Now we have nothing to eat tonight. But tomorrow is another day. In the morning I will try to find the turtle."

The next day the father walked into the forest. He looked and looked for Turtle. Then he got tired and went home. Do you think he ever found Turtle again?

1. **Do you think the children's father will ever find the turtle again? Why or why not?** (Responses will vary.)

2. **Think about the title of this tale. Do you think Turtle is clever? Explain your answer.** (Responses will vary.)

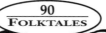

A Measure of Spice

by Kelly Musselman

PURPOSE FOR LISTENING: to enjoy and appreciate a folktale

READ-ALOUD TIP: Display a measuring cup and two containers of different sizes. After reading the story, invite volunteers to experiment by pouring the same amount of water into each container.

It came to pass that the ruler of a faraway kingdom obtained a large quantity of a precious spice. Being a fair ruler, he invited all his subjects to his palace to receive a share of the seasoning. They had only to supply a container in which to carry home their portion.

> Have students set a purpose for listening.

A merchant who dearly loved the taste of this spice decided to bring along the biggest container he had, a fine chest inlaid with precious stones.

The merchant stood in line with the rest of the king's subjects, dreaming of all the dishes he would prepare with his share of the spice. When the merchant's turn came, the king's servant poured a measure of the spice into the chest.

"What?" cried the man. "Is this all I am to receive? But see the fine large chest I have brought to fill."

"That is all. I am sorry," said the servant, going on to the next person in line.

The dissatisfied merchant took his chest and sat under a tree. He looked down at his pitiful pile of spice, which did not even cover the bottom of the chest.

Then he noticed an old woman carrying a simple basket made of reeds. The woman walked slowly, for the basket was filled almost to overflowing.

"Why, she has received much more spice than I!" complained the man to himself. "I will offer to exchange my meager portion, along with this beautiful chest, for her basketful. Then *I* shall have more spice."

Why did the merchant believe the old woman had received more spice than he had?

The merchant called to the old woman and proposed an exchange of his nearly empty chest for her simple, but quite full, basket. The woman nodded in agreement, and the man walked off proudly with his heaping basket of spice, planning many sumptuous meals.

> *Sumptuous* means "very expensive."

The old woman took the fine chest home. She emptied the spice from the large chest into another reed basket the same size as the one she had just given away to the merchant. The seasoning filled the small basket almost to overflowing, and the woman now had a fine chest in addition to her share of the spice.

1. **Why does the old woman agree to trade her basket of spice for the merchant's chest?** (Possible response: The old woman knows that both hold the same amount of spice, and the chest is worth more than her basket.)

2. **Do you believe that "bigger is not always better"? Why or why not?** (Responses will vary.)

The Billy Goat and the Vegetable Garden

a story from Latin America
retold by Lucía M. González

PURPOSE FOR LISTENING: **to enjoy and appreciate a folktale**

READ-ALOUD TIP: **Use different voices for the old woman, the old man, the goat, and the ant.**

> Have students set a purpose for listening.

Once there was a very old woman and a very old man who lived on a farm. They shared a vegetable garden in which they grew tomatoes, lettuce, peppers, potatoes, beans, and plantains. They spent hours working in their garden and planning all the delicious dishes they were going to make with their vegetables.

One morning, a billy goat came into their garden and began eating up all the vegetables.

"Look!" cried the little old woman. "That billy goat is going to eat up everything in our garden. What shall we do?"

"Don't worry," said the little old man. "I can make him go away if I speak to him very, very nicely."

So he went down to the field where the billy goat was eating and he patted it on its back. "*Buenos días* (BWEH-nos DEE-ahs), Señor Billy Goat," he said. "Good morning. Please do not eat up our garden. You are so young and strong, and we are so old and weak. Surely you can find food somewhere else. Please go away."

> Why do you think the old man is being so polite to the billy goat?

But before the old man finished talking, the rude Señor Billy Goat's legs swung up in the air and his head bent low. Then he turned and charged at the old man with his horns!

"¡*Ay* (AHYEE), *Mujer!* (moo-HAIR) ¡*Mujer!*" the old man cried out to his wife, running up the hill as fast as he could. "Open the door, please! The billy goat is after me!"

The little old man ran inside the house, shut the door, and began to cry.

"Do not cry," said his wife. "Perhaps a little tact and style is what he needs. I will go to him and make him go away." So she went down the hill to the field to have a talk with the billy goat herself.

Quietly, she tiptoed to where the billy goat was eating. Bowing low, she whispered, "*Buenos días*, Señor Billy Goat. A gracious good morning to you, kind sir, and I am sorry to disturb your breakfast. This fine food you are eating must have taken some poor farmer a long, long time and much hard work to till the soil, and to plant the seeds, and to pull the weeds. But now, I have come to ask you — "

That was as far as she got, for the billy goat tired of her chatter and turned upon her. His legs swung up in the air and his head was bent low and he charged at her with his horns.

The old woman ran. Up the hill she went, crying, "*Ay*, Husband! Open the door, please! The billy goat is after me!" And she, too, tumbled inside the little house.

As soon as she was safely inside, they both began to cry. For they had been as polite and tactful as anyone could ever be. But that mean-spirited billy goat still got the best of them. Then suddenly, something tickled the little old man's ear. He shook his head to get rid of it and, as he did, down dropped a little red ant.

"I have come to help you," said the little ant. "I can make Señor Billy Goat go away from your garden."

"*You?*" cried the little old woman. "You are so small, what can you do? How can *you* help *us*?"

Ay is used as an exclamation in Spanish. *Mujer* means "woman" or "wife" in Spanish.

Tact is the ability to say something unpleasant in a way that will not hurt the feelings of others.

What do you think the billy goat will do next? Why do you think so?

"Just watch me," said the ant. "You are being too nice to that bully. I can speak to him in the only language he understands."

And with that, the little ant crawled out of the house, through the field, and over to the billy goat. The goat didn't even see the little ant as he crawled up his hind leg, across his back, straight up to his ear — and stung him!

"¡Ay!" cried the billy goat.

The little ant now crawled to the other ear and stung him.

"¡Ay!" cried the billy goat again.

Then the little ant crawled up his back and down again — stinging him all over as he crawled along!

"¡Ay, ay, ay, ay, ay!" the billy goat cried. "I have stepped in an anthill! If I don't get out of this garden at once, these ants will eat me alive!"

Quickly, he jumped up into the air and ran out of the garden as fast as he could.

> Do you think the billy goat learns a lesson? Explain.

The little old man and the little old woman gave many thanks to that brave and clever little red ant for saving their vegetable garden, and they always made sure he had plenty to eat. They spent many hours that fall harvesting their beautiful ripe vegetables and talking about the delicious dishes they were going to prepare.

And what about that billy goat? Well, for all anyone knows, he hasn't gone near that vegetable garden to this very day!

1. **The ant stings the billy goat to make him go away. Do you think hurting someone is the right way to handle a problem? Explain.** (Responses will vary.)

2. **Were you surprised that a tiny ant could solve such a big problem? Why or why not?** (Responses will vary.)

Songs

Take Me Out to the Ball Game

words by Jack Norworth
music by Albert Von Tilzer

PURPOSE FOR LISTENING: to participate in singing songs

READ-ALOUD TIP: Sing this song, or play a recording of it.

With enthusiasm   *Arranged by Randa Kirshbaum*

Take me out to the ball game;

Take me out to the crowd. Buy me some

Have you ever been to a baseball game? Describe what it felt like to be there. (Responses will vary.)

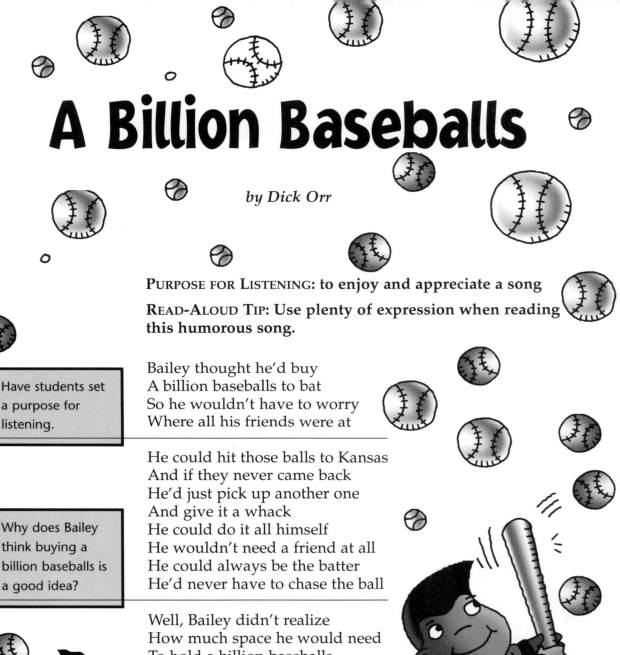

A Billion Baseballs

by Dick Orr

PURPOSE FOR LISTENING: to enjoy and appreciate a song

READ-ALOUD TIP: Use plenty of expression when reading this humorous song.

Have students set a purpose for listening.

Bailey thought he'd buy
A billion baseballs to bat
So he wouldn't have to worry
Where all his friends were at

He could hit those balls to Kansas
And if they never came back
He'd just pick up another one
And give it a whack
He could do it all himself
He wouldn't need a friend at all
He could always be the batter
He'd never have to chase the ball

Why does Bailey think buying a billion baseballs is a good idea?

Well, Bailey didn't realize
How much space he would need
To hold a billion baseballs
Is a lot of space indeed
If he didn't stack them
Just laid them on the ground
It would make a giant square
That was eighty miles around

Well, he didn't have that kind of room
He'd put them in the yard
He'd stack them up against the house
That couldn't be too hard
He took his father's measuring stick
He had to be precise
He measured every inch of space
In fact he did it twice

The yard was thirty feet by thirty feet
A perfect space indeed
But then he had to figure out
How tall a ladder he would need
He added and subtracted
And then he said, "Oh my,
I will need a ladder
That is thirty miles high"

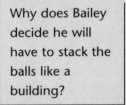

He could stack them like a building
And build steps into the walls
It'd be eleven thousand stories high
Made completely out of balls
He'd have to stack them carefully
Or the balls would all fall down

And then he'd really have a mess
With baseballs all over town

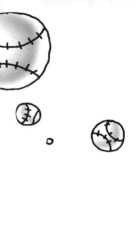

Why does Bailey
decide he will
have to stack the
balls like a
building?

Let's see, if he stacked the balls 1 per second, he could stack sixty in a minute, three thousand six hundred in an hour, eighty-six thousand four hundred in a day, thirty-one million five hundred and thirty-six thousand in a year — it would take him at least thirty-four and one half years to stack the balls. He'd be forty-four years old. He didn't have that kind of time. He would need help.

He'd call up every friend he knew
He was sure they'd help him stack
They could even bring their baseball bats
And they could take a whack
They'd stack a few and hit a few
Unless of course it rained
They could even choose up teams
And play a baseball game

Then he began to understand
The concept of it all

A *concept* is an idea. What is the idea that Bailey begins to understand at the end of the song?

If you have at least two people
You only need one ball . . .
One person hits the baseball
It's the other's turn to catch
Then everybody gets a turn
And the ball keeps coming back

Could someone really have a billion baseballs? (Possible response: You could not have that many baseballs because you would have nowhere to keep them.)

Doing Dishes

by Gary Soto

PURPOSE FOR LISTENING: to compare experiences and ideas with those of others

READ-ALOUD TIP: Encourage children to use the sensory details in this song to build a mental picture of the scene.

Last night

We had one pot

And three dishes.

Tonight, when it's my turn

To throw my hands

Into suds

Have students set a purpose for listening.

We have a stack

Of plates

The color of chickens,

White and red.

That's what we

Had tonight — chicken *mole,*
(mo-LAY) (muelle fricassee of meat with chili sauce)

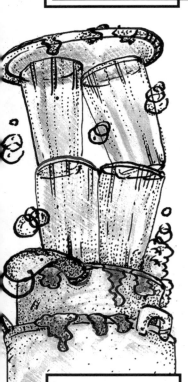

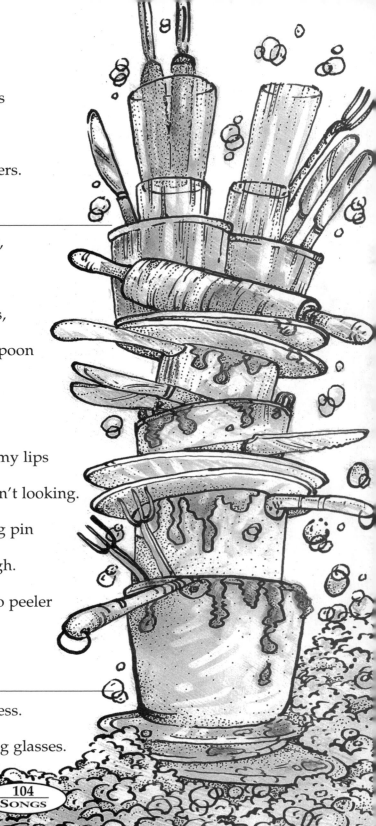

A messy meal

That leaves stains

On your mouth

And greedy fingers.

We have plates.

We have six pots,

A jangle of

Forks and knives,

And a wooden spoon

That paddled

Through sauce

And docked on my lips

When Mom wasn't looking.

We have a rolling pin

Sticky with dough.

We have a potato peeler

And a pie pan

When the flan

Set in its sweetness.

We have drinking glasses.

How does the boy in the poem feel about doing dishes? How do you know?

Flan is a baked-custard dessert with a caramel sauce.

I pump the suds

And scrub,

My sponge raking

The *mole* sauce,

The *frijoles* (free-HO-lays),

The *arroz* (ah-ROHZ),

The *papas* (PAH-pahz).

The dishwater

Turns orange,

And suds flatten.

I drain the water

And start again,

A curl of steam

Licking my eyebrows.

I wipe my eyebrow.

I pump my sponge.

I sweat over the suds

And wail inside

Because it's boring.

Frijoles is the Spanish word for "beans." *Arroz* is the Spanish word for "rice." *Papas* is the Spanish word for "potatoes."

I could be doing

Nothing right now,

Or reading a magazine,

Which is almost

Like doing nothing.

But I scrub and rinse,

And am here

Leaning my belly

Against the sink

For hours, days, years. . . .

When I finally

Pull my hands

From the water,

They're puckered and old

— that's how long!

Tell about a time when you felt the same way about completing a chore or a task as this boy does about doing the dishes. (Responses will vary.)

Poems

Nine Gold Medals

by David Roth

PURPOSE FOR LISTENING: to respond appropriately to questions

READ-ALOUD TIP: Read this moving poem with a measured pace.

The athletes had come from all over the country
To run for the gold, for the silver and bronze
Many weeks and months of training
All coming down to these games

The spectators gathered around the old field
To cheer on all the young women and men
The final event of the day was approaching
Excitement grew high to begin

The blocks were all lined up for those who would use
them
The hundred-yard dash was the race to be run
There were nine resolved athletes in back of the starting
line
Poised for the sound of the gun

The signal was given, the pistol exploded
And so did the runners all charging ahead
But the smallest among them, he stumbled and staggered
And fell to the asphalt instead

He gave out a cry in frustration and anguish
His dreams and his efforts all dashed in the dirt
But as sure as I'm standing here telling this story
The same goes for what next occurred

The eight other runners pulled up on their heels
The ones who had trained for so long to compete
One by one they all turned around and went back to help
 him
And brought the young boy to his feet

> What usually
> happens when
> one of the runners
> in a race falls?
> What do you
> think will happen
> in this race?

Then all the nine runners joined hands and continued
The hundred-yard dash now reduced to a walk
And a banner above that said "Special Olympics"
Could not have been more on the mark

That's how the race ended, with nine gold medals
They came to the finish line holding hands still
And a standing ovation and nine beaming faces
Said more than these words ever will

> People with
> mental and
> physical disabilities
> take part in the
> *Special Olympics.*

**How is this race different from others you have seen or
read about?** (Responses will vary.)

Limericks

compiled by Warren Lyfick

PURPOSE FOR LISTENING: **to enjoy and appreciate limericks**

READ-ALOUD TIP: Read each of the limericks several times so that children can visualize the images.

There was an old man in a tree,
Whose whiskers were lovely to see;
    But the birds of the air
    Pluck'd them perfectly bare,
To make themselves nests in that tree.

Pluck means "to pull out."

Edward Lear

A cheerful old bear at the zoo,
Could always find something to do.
    When it bored him to go,
    On a walk to and fro,
He reversed it, and walked fro and to.

To and fro means "moving first in one direction and then back again."

Anonymous

There was a young farmer of Leeds,
Who swallowed six packets of seeds.
    It soon came to pass
    He was covered with grass,
And he couldn't sit down for the weeds.

Anonymous

Which limerick did you like best?
Why? (Responses will vary.)

Helping

by Shel Silverstein

PURPOSE FOR LISTENING: to interpret and evaluate

READ-ALOUD TIP: Emphasize the alliteration in this poem.

Agatha Fry, she made a pie,
And Christopher John helped bake it.
Christopher John, he mowed the lawn,
And Agatha Fry helped rake it.
Zachary Zugg took out the rug,
And Jennifer Joy helped shake it.
And Jennifer Joy, she made a toy,
And Zachary Zugg helped break it.

And some kind of help
Is the kind of help
That helping's all about.
And some kind of help
Is the kind of help
We all can do without.

What are the two kinds of helping described in this poem? (Possible response: The first kind of helping helps do something good. The second kind of helping helps do something bad.)

America, the Beautiful Home of Dinosaurs

by Jeff Moss

PURPOSE FOR LISTENING: to gain information

READ-ALOUD TIP: Display a map of the United States, and ask volunteers to point out each state as you read its name aloud in the poem.

> The *Cretaceous* period was the time in history when the dinosaurs began to disappear.

In the time we call Cretaceous (kreh-TAY-shuss),
Skies were beautiful and spacious
But there were no deer or antelope at play.
Yet *Triceratops* (try-SER-uh-tops) were roaming
Through the hills of old Wyoming —
There were dinosaurs throughout the U.S.A.

Great *Tyrannosaurus rexes* (tie-RAN-uh-saw-russ REX-uhz)
Lived deep in the heart of Texas,
Though the folks from Texas sure are glad they've gone.
Stegosaurs (STEG-uh-sawrs) roamed Colorado
("Eat those plants!" was once their motto).
And in South Dakota lived *Iguanodon* (ig-WAN-uh-don).

You can bet a big banana
Allosaurs (AL-uh-sawrz) in old Montana
Left their massive footprints in the ancient stones.
Scuttelosaurus (scoo-TELL-o-saw-russ), itty-bitty,
Made her home near Salt Lake City
Out in Utah where they found her little bones.

Dinos lived in North Dakota,
Massachusetts, Minnesota—
Old New Jersey was the home of hadrosaur (HAD-ruh-sawr)
And it's really quite amazing
When you think of dinos grazing
On your lawn two hundred million years before.

So let's cheer them in a chorus—
Every dinosaur or saurus—
They're American as home-baked apple pies.
And our last historic fact'll
Be a large pterodactyl (ter-uh-DAK-til)
Making circles in our beautiful spacious skies.

The words *Eat those plants* show that Stegosaurs were plant-eating dinosaurs.

What did you learn about dinosaurs from listening to this poem? (Possible response: Dinosaurs once lived all over the United States—Triceratops in Wyoming, Tyrannosaurus rex in Texas, Stegosaurs in Colorado, Iguanodon in South Dakota, Allosaurs in Montana, Scuttelosaurus in Utah, and hadrosaur in New Jersey.)

Where Go the Boats?

by Robert Louis Stevenson

PURPOSE FOR LISTENING: to listen critically to interpret

READ-ALOUD TIP: Read this poem several times so
children can visualize the images.

Dark brown is the river,
  Golden is the sand.
It flows along for ever,
  With trees on either hand.

Green leaves a-floating,
  Castles of the foam,
Boats of mine a-boating—
  Where will all come home?

On goes the river,
  And out past the mill,
Away down the valley,
  Away down the hill.

Away down the river,
  A hundred miles or more,
Other little children
  Shall bring my boats ashore.

> What "flows
> along for ever"?

**What does the child in the poem think might happen
to his boats?** (Possible response: He thinks that other children
might take his boats out of the water farther down the river.)

114
POEMS

Good Company

by Leonard Clark

PURPOSE FOR LISTENING: to enjoy and appreciate a poem

READ-ALOUD TIP: Read this lyrical poem in a thoughtful tone of voice.

I sleep in a room at the top of the house
With a flea, and a fly, and a soft-scratching mouse,
And a spider that hangs by a thread from the ceiling,
Who gives me each day such a curious feeling
When I watch him at work on the beautiful weave
Of his web that's so fine I can hardly believe
It won't all end up in such terrible tangles,
For he sways as he weaves, and spins as he dangles.

I cannot get up to that spider, I know,
And I hope he won't get down to me here below,
And yet when I wake in the chill morning air
I'd miss him if he were not still swinging there,
For I have in my room such good company,
There's him, and the mouse, and the fly, and the flea.

Spider webs are made from silky thread that the spider weaves into a pattern. The spider can use some of the same thread as a rope ladder to go up and down in the air.

Would you think of a flea, a fly, a mouse, or a spider as good company? Why or why not? (Responses will vary.)

Old Crocodile

by Sydnie Meltzer Kleinhenz

PURPOSE FOR LISTENING: to enjoy and appreciate a poem

READ-ALOUD TIP: Display a photograph of a crocodile as you read this poem.

The Sudan folk along the Nile—

They joke about Old Crocodile.

At basking time, he jives and croons.

But lions do not like the tunes!

And monkeys scamper off a mile.

And tsetses fly away in style.

And sighing hippopotami

Decide it's time to say, "Good-bye!"

Hyenas stride, and pythons slide,

And zebras find a place to hide.

Most everybody tries to flee . . .

Old Crocodile sings way off-key!

Basking time is the time when an animal lies in and enjoys the warmth of the sun. *Jives and croons* means moves and sings with music."

According to the poem, why do all the animals run away when it's basking time for Old Crocodile? (Possible response: The crocodile likes to sing at basking time, and his singing is off-key.)

Since Hanna Moved Away

by Judith Viorst

PURPOSE FOR LISTENING: **to enjoy and appreciate a poem**

READ-ALOUD TIP: Use plenty of expression as you read the
heartfelt lament of a lonely friend.

The tires on my bike are flat.
The sky is grouchy gray.
At least it sure feels like that
Since Hanna moved away.

Chocolate ice cream tastes like prunes.
December's come to stay.
They've taken back the Mays and Junes
Since Hanna moved away.

Flowers smell like halibut.
Velvet feels like hay.
Every handsome dog's a mutt
Since Hanna moved away.

> *Halibut* is a kind
> of fish. Why do
> flowers smell like
> fish to the speaker
> in this poem?

Nothing's fun to laugh about.
Nothing's fun to play.
They call me, but I won't come out
Since Hanna moved away.

**What has happened to make the child in this poem
feel sad?** (Possible response: The narrator's friend Hanna has
moved away.)

The Key of the Kingdom

Anonymous

PURPOSE FOR LISTENING: to enjoy and appreciate a poem

READ-ALOUD TIP: Read the first stanza of this cumulative poem slowly, stressing the nouns in each line. Then read the second stanza at a faster and faster pace.

This is the key of the kingdom:
In that kingdom is a city;

Have students set
a purpose for
listening.

In that city is a town;
In that town is a street;
In that street there winds a lane;
In that lane there is a yard;
In that yard there is a house;
In that house there waits a room;
In that room an empty bed,
And on that bed a basket—
A basket of sweet flowers
   Of flowers, of flowers;
   A basket of sweet flowers.

Flowers in a basket;
Basket on the bed;
Bed in the room;
Room in the house;
House in the yard;
Yard in the winding lane;
Lane in the street;
Street in the town;
Town in the city;
City in the kingdom—
This is the key of the kingdom.
   Of the kingdom this is the key.

Put your pencil on your desk. Tell about your pencil the way the poet told about the flowers in the basket. (Possible response: pencil, desk, classroom, school, neighborhood, town, state, United States, Earth)

The POWER SHOVEL

by Rowena Bennett

PURPOSE FOR LISTENING: to listen responsively to a poem

READ-ALOUD TIP: Use a slightly ominous tone as you read this poem.

The power digger
Is much bigger
   Than the biggest beast I know.
He snorts and roars
Like the dinosaurs
   That lived long years ago.

He crouches low
   On his tractor paws
And scoops the dirt up
   With his jaws;
Then swings his long
   Stiff neck around
And spits it out
   Upon the ground.

Oh, the power digger
Is much bigger
   Than the biggest beast I know.
He snorts and roars
Like the dinosaurs
   That lived long years ago.

Do you agree with the poet that big construction machines are like dinosaurs? Why or why not? (Responses will vary.)

De KOVEN

by Gwendolyn Brooks

PURPOSE FOR LISTENING: to enjoy and appreciate a poem

READ-ALOUD TIP: Read this short poem several times so listeners can create a mental picture of the star.

You are a dancy little thing,
You are a rascal, star!
You seem to be so near to me,
And yet you are so far.

> What is this poem about? How do you know?

If I could get you in my hands
You'd never get away.
I'd keep you with me always.
You'd shine both night and day.

Do you like looking at stars as much as the child in this poem does? How do stars make you feel?
(Responses will vary.)

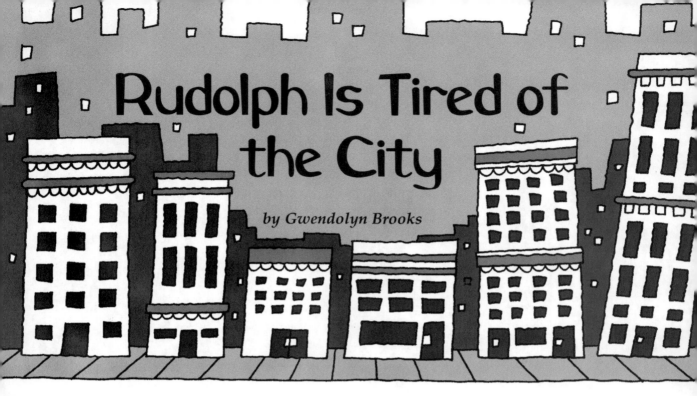

Rudolph Is Tired of the City

by Gwendolyn Brooks

PURPOSE FOR LISTENING: to connect experiences with those of others

READ-ALOUD TIP: Read this poem using an expressive voice.

These buildings are too close to me.
I'd like to PUSH away.
I'd like to live in the country,
And spread my arms all day.

I'd like to spread my breath out, too—
As farmers' sons and daughters do.

I'd tend the cows and chickens.
I'd do the other chores.
Then, all the hours left I'd go
A-SPREADING out-of-doors.

Do you ever daydream about places far away? Tell about a time you wished you could live someplace else.
(Responses will vary.)

Nonfiction

The *Eagle* Has Landed

by William J. Bennett

PURPOSE FOR LISTENING: to gain information

READ-ALOUD TIP: Add another dimension to this story by displaying photographs taken by the *Apollo 11* astronauts.

Curiosity about the unknown led early voyagers to our shores. They called it the New World back then. Nearly five hundred years later, that same spirit led Americans to a more distant world—the moon.

It was one of humankind's oldest dreams. For hundreds of years, people had looked to the sky and wondered if they would ever walk on the moon.

"Never." Some shook their heads. "It can't be done."

"Someday," the dreamers insisted.

Have students set a purpose for listening.

One July morning in 1969, three Americans, named Neil Armstrong, Mike Collins, and Buzz Aldrin, climbed into a tiny space capsule atop a giant rocket and waited for a countdown. Five huge engines thundered to life. Flames and smoke poured across the launchpad and Apollo 11 rode a column of fire into the sky.

"We have liftoff!" announced a voice on the ground.

No one knew if the men on board would ever make it back.

Gazing down, the astronauts saw the wide curve of the Earth with its spreading seas and lush forests and drifting clouds. Through the capsule's window, they watched their planet shrink into a blue and white sphere. The spaceship rolled and the Earth slipped silently out of sight.

For three days, the *Apollo 11* astronauts hurtled into the blackness of space. A second sphere, this one gray and lifeless, swelled until it filled their window. Then they were circling the moon.

Hurtled means "moved with great speed."

Neil Armstrong and Buzz Aldrin squeezed through a hatch and crawled into a boxy, four-legged landing vehicle named the *Eagle*. In this fragile craft they would try to drop to the moon's surface while Mike Collins flew high above, ready to rescue his friends if anything went wrong.

The radio hissed and crackled. A voice called from Mission Control in Houston, Texas, a quarter million miles away, "You are go for separation."

Slowly the *Eagle* and the mother ship backed away from each other. The lander floated free.

"The *Eagle* has wings," Neil Armstrong reported to Earth. Inside the cramped cabin, he and Aldrin watched the ghostly moonscape rolling by.

What did Neil Armstrong mean when he said, "The *Eagle* has wings"?

Everything was ready. Another order came from Houston. "You are go for powered descent."

The engine fired and the *Eagle* began its short downward journey. Armstrong nodded and Aldrin grinned to himself. They were going to land on the moon.

But suddenly bells began to clang inside the tiny craft. Something was wrong.

"Give us a reading on that alarm," Armstrong called back to Earth. His voice was suddenly strained. If it was a serious problem, they would have to turn back.

"Hang tight," came the instruction.

The *Eagle*'s computer, which was guiding the ship, had signaled that it was having trouble handling all its chores.

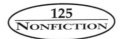

The astronauts' hearts thumped hard inside their chests. The gray face of the moon rushed toward them. There was nothing to do but wait for Houston to study the problem and tell them whether to keep going or abandon the mission.

Then came the command. "*Eagle*, you are go for landing. Go!"

The spacecraft continued downward.

Armstrong turned to the window to look for their landing zone. He did not like what he saw. They were not where they were supposed to be.

The computer was programmed to steer the ship to a flat, smooth place for a landing. But it had overshot its target. They were plunging straight toward an area littered with deadly rocks and craters.

A light blinked on the control panel. They were running out of landing fuel.

How do you think the astronauts felt?

There was no time to waste. Armstrong gripped the hand controller and took command from the computer. He had to find a place where they could set down, fast, or they would have to fire their rockets and return to space.

Gently he brought the *Eagle* under his control. The lander hovered as Armstrong searched the ground below for a level spot.

"Sixty seconds," the voice from Mission Control warned. Sixty seconds of fuel left.

Balanced on a cone of fire, the *Eagle* scooted over rocky ridges and yawning craters.

There was no place to land!

"Thirty seconds!"

Now there was no turning back. If the engines gulped the last of the landing fuel, there would be no time to fire the rockets that could take them back into orbit. They would crash.

What problem did Neil Armstrong have when he tried to land the *Eagle*?

The landing craft swooped across boulder fields as its pilot hunted, judged, and committed. Flames shot down as the *Eagle* dropped the last few feet. Dust that had lain still for a billion years flew up and swallowed the craft.

Back on Earth, millions of people held their breaths and waited. They prayed and listened.

Then Neil Armstrong's faint voice came crackling across the gulf of space. "Houston, Tranquillity Base here. The *Eagle* has landed."

In a short while a hatch on the lander opened. A man in a bulky space suit backed down nine rungs of a ladder and placed his foot on the gray lunar soil. People all over the world watched the fuzzy black-and-white images on their television screens. They leaned toward their sets to catch the first words spoken by Neil Armstrong from the surface of the moon.

"That's one small step for man, one giant leap for mankind."

> Why did millions of people on Earth hold their breaths?

A few minutes later Buzz Aldrin crawled out of the *Eagle* to join his comrade. Together the astronauts planted a flag.

It would never flap in a breeze on the airless moon, so a stiff wire held it out from its pole. Aldrin stepped back and saluted the Stars and Stripes.

America had made the age-old dream come true. When they departed, our astronauts left behind a plaque that will always remain. Its words proclaim:

> What do you think Neil Armstrong meant when he said, "That's one small step for man, one giant leap for mankind"?

HERE MEN FROM THE PLANET EARTH
FIRST SET FOOT UPON THE MOON
JULY, 1969 A.D.
WE CAME IN PEACE FOR ALL MANKIND

1. **Would you like to have been part of the astronaut team aboard the *Eagle*? Why or why not?** (Responses will vary.)

2. **If you could interview the astronauts who were aboard the *Eagle*, what would you ask them?** (Responses will vary.)

Koko's Story

by Dr. Francine Patterson

PURPOSE FOR LISTENING: to gain information

READ-ALOUD TIP: While reading this selection, pause before saying each of the words Koko learns and signs.

Koko was born at the San Francisco Zoo on the fourth of July in 1971. She was named Hanabi-Ko, a Japanese word meaning "fireworks child," but everyone called her Koko.

She was three months old when I first saw her, a tiny gorilla clinging to her mother's back. I asked the zoo director if I could try to teach her sign language. He said no.

> *Sign language* is a way of communicating with people who cannot hear.

I didn't get my chance to work with her until one year later. Soon after I had first seen Koko, she became very sick. A terrible illness had spread through the gorilla colony. Koko almost died, but was nursed back to health by doctors and staff at the zoo. Her mother had been unable to care for her, and now Koko lived at the Children's Zoo. She was healthy again, but could not yet live among older gorillas.

I started visiting Koko at the zoo every day. At first, I didn't think Koko liked me. She ignored me. She bit me when I tried to pick her up. Slowly, though, because I never failed to come see her every day, Koko began to trust me.

Each morning, I would carry her around the zoo on my back to visit the other animals. When we passed the baby elephant, Koko would cling to me tightly, scared by the loud trumpeting noise the elephant made whenever we went near.

I first attempted to teach Koko just three words in sign language: *drink, food,* and *more.* I taught the zoo assistants who helped in the nursery to form the sign "food" with their hands. They used this sign whenever they gave Koko anything to eat.

What does the author do to earn Koko's trust?

"Drink," I signed each time I gave Koko her bottle.

I formed her small hand into the sign for "drink," too.

One morning, about a month after I began working with Koko, I was slicing fruit for her snack. Koko was watching me.

What do you think Koko will do?

"Food," she signed.

I couldn't believe my eyes.

"Food," she clearly signed again. Koko had communicated with me! I wanted to jump for joy. Koko could sense I was happy with her. She became so excited that she grabbed a bucket, plunked it over her head, and ran wildly around the playroom.

By age two, Koko's signs were more than just simple, one-word requests like "up," "drink," and "more." Now Koko was learning signs quickly and stringing them together.

"There mouth, mouth-you there," Koko signed when she wanted me to blow fog on the nursery window to draw in with our fingers.

"Pour that hurry drink hurry," she signed when she was thirsty.

Koko had a big birthday party when she turned three. One of her presents was a pair of toy binoculars.

"Look," she signed, marching proudly with the binoculars around her neck.

She carefully ate almost all of her birthday cake with a spoon. But when it came time for the last bite, Koko couldn't resist. She scooped the cake up with her hand and stuffed it into her mouth.

"More eat," she signed.

On her birthday, we forgave her for such table manners.

> What does Koko talk about most? Why do you think Koko does this?

1. **How does the author teach Koko to use sign language?** (Possible response: The author and the other people at the zoo signed the same three words whenever they fed Koko. Then the author showed Koko how to make the same signs.)

2. **How is Koko like a human two- or three-year-old?** (Responses will vary.)

Teddy's Bear

by Janeen R. Adil

PURPOSE FOR LISTENING: gain information.

READ-ALOUD TIP: Add another dimension to this story by having a teddy bear on your desk as you read this story.

> Have students set a purpose for listening.

Theodore "Teddy" Roosevelt, America's twenty-sixth president, was famous for accomplishing many important things while he was in office. Something he *didn't* do, however, made him just as famous. And because of it, one of the best-loved toys ever created was named after him.

In November 1902, President Roosevelt traveled south to settle a boundary dispute between Mississippi and Louisiana. While he was there, he took some time off to go bear hunting. Several reporters and a well-known newspaper artist named Clifford Berryman joined the president's hunting trip.

> A *boundary dispute* is an argument about state or county borders.

The hunters didn't have much luck. Finally, on the last day of the hunt, the president spotted a bear. As he carefully aimed his rifle, the animal turned around. It was only a cub! Teddy Roosevelt loved to hunt, but he refused to shoot this frightened little bear.

Clifford Berryman thought this was a wonderful opportunity for a drawing. He sketched a cartoon of President Roosevelt turning his back on the cub, unwilling to shoot the small creature. Soon Berryman's black-and-white drawing was appearing in newspapers all over the country. People everywhere liked the cartoon and thought it showed the president to be a kind-hearted man.

One of those who saw and enjoyed the drawing was Morris Michtom, a candy store owner in Brooklyn, New York. He and his wife, Rose, knew how to make stuffed toys, and the cartoon gave them an idea. The Michtoms found some brown plush fabric and cut out pieces for a bear with movable arms and legs. Then they sewed and stuffed the bear and added buttons for its eyes.

Why was the first teddy bear made?

The Michtoms placed the new toy bear, a copy of Berryman's cartoon, and a sign that read "Teddy's Bear" in the front window of their store. The bear sold quickly, and so did the next few that the Michtoms made. When Morris saw how popular the bears were, he knew he would need the president's permission to continue using his name.

Morris wrote a letter to the White House and received a handwritten reply from Theodore Roosevelt himself. "I don't think my name is likely to be worth much in the bear business," the president wrote, "but you are welcome to use it." So the Michtoms went to work, making one teddy bear after another.

Why did Morris Michtom write to President Roosevelt?

Since Rose and Morris made the bears themselves and still had a candy store to manage, they produced the bears slowly at first. Eventually they closed the candy store, and the Michtom family business became the Ideal Toy Company, one of America's biggest toymakers. Soon other companies in the United States and Europe were producing bears of all shapes, sizes, and prices. Some of the most beautiful stuffed bears were made in Germany by Margarete Steiff and her workers.

In just a few years, teddy bears had become extremely popular. Other items related to the stuffed bears were sold, too. Not only could one buy clothing for a teddy bear, but there were also bear puzzles, bear books, bear games, bear banks—all sorts of toys and amusements! Teddy bears had become as important to children as blocks, dolls, and balls had already been for generations.

Today teddy bears remain a favorite of boys and girls everywhere. Many adults love to collect and display them, too. Hundreds of millions of teddy bears have been produced since Teddy Roosevelt's hunting trip so many years ago. Who could have guessed that the story of an unlucky president and a frightened bear cub would have such a happy ending?

1. **Why do you think President Roosevelt refused to shoot the bear?** (Possible responses will vary.)

2. **Do you think the Michtoms were creative people? Explain.** (Possible responses will vary.)

Johnny Appleseed

by Steven Kellogg

PURPOSE FOR LISTENING: to gain information

READ-ALOUD TIP: Read slowly to help children build mental images of the events that take place in this story.

John Chapman, who later became known as Johnny Appleseed, was born on September 26, 1774, when the apples on the trees surrounding his home in Leominster, Massachusetts, were as red as the autumn leaves.

> Have students set a purpose for listening.

John's first years were hard. His father left the family to fight in the Revolutionary War, and his mother and his baby brother both died before his second birthday.

By the time John turned six, his father had remarried and settled in Longmeadow, Massachusetts. Within a decade their little house was overflowing with ten more children.

Nearby was an apple orchard. Like most early American families, the Chapmans picked their apples in the fall, stored them in the cellar for winter eating, and used them to make sauces, cider, vinegar, and apple butter. John loved to watch the spring blossoms slowly turn into the glowing fruit of autumn.

Watching the apples grow inspired in John a love of all nature. He often escaped from his boisterous household to the tranquil woods. The animals sensed his gentleness and trusted him.

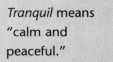

Tranquil means "calm and peaceful."

As soon as John was old enough to leave home, he set out to explore the vast wilderness to the west. When he reached the Allegheny Mountains, he cleared a plot of land and planted a small orchard with the pouch of apple seeds he had carried with him.

John walked hundreds of miles through the Pennsylvania forest, living like the Indians he befriended on the trail. As he traveled, he cleared the land for many more orchards. He was sure the pioneer families would be arriving before long, and he looked forward to supplying them with apple trees.

What did John do for the pioneer families?

When a storm struck, he found shelter in a hollow log or built a lean-to. On clear nights he stretched out under the stars.

Over the next few years, John continued to visit and care for his new orchards. The winters slowed him down, but he survived happily on a diet of butternuts.

One spring he met a band of men who boasted that they could lick their weight in wildcats. They were amazed to hear that John wouldn't hurt an animal.

They challenged John to compete at wrestling, the favorite frontier sport. He suggested a more practical contest—a tree-chopping match. The woodsmen eagerly agreed.

When the sawdust settled, there was no question about who had come out on top.

How did the land for his largest orchard get cleared so quickly?

John was pleased that the land for his largest orchard had been so quickly cleared. He thanked the exhausted woodsmen for their help and began planting.

During the next few years, John continued to move westward. Whenever he ran out of apple seeds, he hiked to the eastern cider presses to replenish his supply. Before long, John's plantings were spread across the state of Ohio.

A *cider press* is a machine that makes cider by pressing the juice out of apples.

Meanwhile, pioneer families were arriving in search of homesites and farmland. John had located his orchards on the routes he thought they'd be traveling. As he had hoped, the settlers were eager to buy his young trees.

John went out of his way to lend a helping hand to his new neighbors. Often he would give his trees away. People affectionately called him Johnny Appleseed, and he began using that name.

He particularly enjoyed entertaining children with tales of his wilderness adventures and stories from the Bible.

In 1812 the British incited the Indians to join them in another war against the Americans. The settlers feared that Ohio would be invaded from Lake Erie.

It grieved Johnny that his friends were fighting each other. But when he saw the smoke of burning cabins, he ran through the night, shouting a warning at every door.

After the war, people urged Johnny to build a house and settle down. He replied that he lived like a king in his wilderness home, and he returned to the forest he loved.

> Why wouldn't Johnny build a house and settle down?

During his long absences, folks enjoyed sharing their recollections of Johnny. They retold his stories and sometimes they even exaggerated them a bit.

Some recalled Johnny sleeping in a treetop hammock and chatting with the birds.

Others remembered that a rattlesnake had attacked his foot. Fortunately, Johnny's feet were as tough as elephant's hide, so the fangs didn't penetrate.

It was said that Johnny had once tended a wounded wolf and then kept him for a pet.

An old hunter swore he'd seen Johnny frolicking with a bear family.

The storytellers outdid each other with tall tales about his feats of survival in the untamed wilderness.

> *Tall tales* are exaggerated stories about real or made-up people.

As the years passed, Ohio became too crowded for Johnny. He moved to the wilds of Indiana, where he continued to clear land for his orchards.

When the settlers began arriving, Johnny recognized some of the children who had listened to his stories. Now they had children of their own.

It made Johnny's old heart glad when they welcomed him as a beloved friend and asked to hear his tales again.

When Johnny passed seventy, it became difficult for him to keep up with his work. Then, in March of 1845, while trudging through a snowstorm near Fort Wayne, Indiana, he became ill for the first time in his life.

Johnny asked for shelter in a settler's cabin, and a few days later he died there.

Curiously, Johnny's stories continued to move westward without him. Folks maintained that they'd seen him in

Illinois or that he'd greeted them in Missouri, Arkansas, or Texas. Others were certain that he'd planted trees on the slopes of the Rocky Mountains or in California's distant valleys.

Even today people still claim they've seen Johnny Appleseed.

> Why do you think Johnny's stories continued to move westward without him?

1. **Why do you think people began to exaggerate the events in the stories they told about Johnny Appleseed?** (Responses will vary.)

2. **If you could interview Johnny Appleseed, what would you ask him?** (Responses will vary.)

Margaret of New Orleans

adapted from Sarah Cone Bryant

PURPOSE FOR LISTENING: to gain information

READ-ALOUD TIP: Display a map of the state of Louisiana, and point out the city of New Orleans.

Throughout our history, countless people have come to this land of opportunity and, receiving much, have given even more in return. Margaret Haughery was one such immigrant. Her life, modest and compelling, is a reminder that charity is among our most honored national traits.

Have students set a purpose for listening.

If you ever go to beautiful New Orleans, someone might take you down to the old part of the city along the wide Mississippi River and show you a statue that stands there. It depicts a woman sitting in a low chair, with her arms around a child who leans against her. The woman is not very pretty. She wears thick shoes and a plain dress. She is stout and short, and her face is square-chinned. But her eyes look at you like your mother's.

This is the statue of a woman named Margaret. Her whole name was Margaret Haughery, but no one in New Orleans remembers her by it, any more than you would think of your sister or your best friend by her full name. She is just Margaret. Born across the ocean in Ireland more than 150 years ago, she came to America when she was just a little girl and grew up here. Her statue is one of the first ever made in our country in honor of a woman.

As a young woman Margaret was all alone in the world. She was poor but strong, and she knew how to work. All day, from morning until evening, she ironed clothes in a laundry. And every day, as she worked by the window, she saw the little children from the nearby orphanage working and playing. They had no mothers or fathers of their own to take care of them. Margaret knew they needed a good friend.

Who is the woman in the statue?

You would hardly think that a poor woman who worked in a laundry could be much of a friend to so many children. But Margaret was. She went straight to the kind Sisters who ran the orphanage and told them she wanted to help the little ones.

What kind of person is Margaret?

So she gave part of her wages every week to the orphanage. She worked so hard that she was able to save some money, too. With this, she bought two cows and a delivery cart. She carried milk to her customers in the little cart every morning. As she went along, she asked for leftover food from hotels and rich houses, and brought it back in the cart to the hungry children in the orphanage. In the very hardest times, that was often all the food the children had.

In spite of her giving, Margaret was so careful and so good at business that she was able to buy more cows and earn more money. With this, she helped build a home for orphan babies. She called it her baby house.

Was Margaret a good business person? How can you tell?

After a time, Margaret had a chance to take over a bakery, and then she became a bread woman instead of a milk woman. She carried the bread just as she had carried the milk, in her cart. And still she kept giving money to the orphanage.

Then a great war came, the Civil War. In all the trouble and fear of that time, Margaret drove her cart. Somehow she always had enough bread to give to the hungry soldiers and to her babies, besides what she sold. And despite all this, she earned enough so that when the war was over she built a big steam factory to make her bread.

By this time everybody in the city knew her. The children all over New Orleans loved her. The businessmen were proud of her. The poor people all came to her for advice. She used to sit at the open door of her office in a calico gown and a little shawl and give a good word to everybody, rich or poor.

Why do you think everybody in New Orleans knew and liked Margaret?

Margaret grew old and, by and by, one day she died. When it was time to read her will, people found that, even with all her giving, she had still saved a great deal of

money—and she had left every cent of it to the orphanages of the city. Each one of them was given something. Whether the children were boys or girls, white or black, Jews or Christians, made no difference, for Margaret always said, "They are all orphans alike." Her splendid will was signed with an X instead of a name, for Margaret had never learned to read or write.

The people of New Orleans said, "She was a mother to the motherless. She was a friend to those who had no friends. She had wisdom greater than schools can teach. We will not let her memory go from us." So they made a statue of her, just as she used to look sitting in her office door or driving in her own little cart. And there it stands today, in memory of the great love and the great power of plain Margaret Haughery of New Orleans.

---

1. **Who was Margaret Haughery? What did you learn about her?** (Possible response: She was a caring and hard-working woman who was a good friend to the children in an orphanage. Margaret saved enough money to help build a home for orphan babies. Later, she bought a bakery and in time built a steam factory to make her bread.)

2. **What made Margaret Haughery such an unusual person?** (Possible response: She never forgot those who were less fortunate than she was.)

Garrett A. Morgan

"A Champion of Public Safety"
born 1877—died 1963

by Wade Hudson

PURPOSE FOR LISTENING: to gain information

READ-ALOUD TIP: While reading this biography, emphasize the name of each of Garrett Morgan's inventions.

On July 24, 1916, there was an explosion in Tunnel Number Five of the Cleveland, Ohio, Water Works. The tunnel lay more than 250 feet below Lake Erie. Thirty-two men were trapped inside the tunnel. Rescuers could not get to the men because the tunnel was filled with dangerous smoke and natural gas.

> Have students set a purpose for listening.

Garrett Morgan and his brother Frank rushed to the site. They put funny-looking masks over their heads. Garrett had made the masks. The masks had long tubes with holes at the end. The long tubes were very important. Smoke, dust, and gas rise, leaving cleaner air closer to the ground. The long tubes could reach the cleaner air.

The two brothers entered the tunnel along with two other men. The masks protected the men. They brought out the other men who were trapped inside the tunnel. But not all of the trapped men had survived.

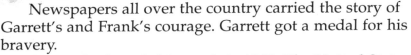

Newspapers all over the country carried the story of Garrett's and Frank's courage. Garrett got a medal for his bravery.

Garrett had made his mask in 1912. The United States government gave Garrett a patent for his invention in

1914. That same year, at a safety and sanitation fair in New York City, Garrett received a gold medal as first prize for his invention. Soon after that, fire departments in some cities began using it. A company was formed to make Garrett's new mask.

Garrett called his invention the "gas inhalator." It sold slowly until the big rescue on July 24, 1916.

Then, people from everywhere wanted to see the funny-looking masks that would let someone walk safely into a smoke-filled tunnel. Fire departments and mining companies were very interested.

In later years, the United States government made some changes to the "gas inhalator." It was then called the gas mask. American soldiers used gas masks during World War I to protect themselves from poisonous gas. They saved many lives.

A *patent* is a piece of paper from the government that says that the inventor is the only person who may make or sell his or her invention.

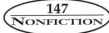

Garrett Morgan was born in Paris, Kentucky. He had ten brothers and sisters. At the age of 14, Garrett moved to Cincinnati, Ohio, where he worked as a handyman. Later, he moved to Cleveland, Ohio. He started a business there.

Garrett Morgan had only an elementary school education. But he was very smart. He liked to invent things.

His first discovery was a chemical to straighten hair. The G. A. Morgan Hair Cream is believed to be the first human hair straightener.

In 1923, Garrett received a patent for a very important invention. Before 1923, there were no traffic lights. Cars and horse-drawn carriages drove through street intersections at their own risk. There were many crashes. Many people were hurt. Garrett invented an electric light signal. The different-colored lights told the driver when to go or stop. That was the beginning of the traffic-light system we still use today.

> What would it be like to drive on busy roads without traffic lights?

After Garrett patented his traffic signal, he sold the rights to the General Electric Corporation for $40,000.00.

Garrett cared very deeply about his fellow black Americans. He felt that the newspapers in Cleveland didn't give fair attention to events in the black community. So he founded the *Cleveland Call* newspaper. It is now called the *Cleveland Call & Post*. Then in 1931, Garrett ran for the city council in Cleveland. He wanted to give black people better representation in city government.

> Garrett Morgan had very little schooling, but the author says he was very smart. How can you tell this is true?

Garrett Morgan lived a long and successful life. He was 86 years old when he died.

1. **What are some of the items that Garrett Morgan invented? What did he do to help people in his community?** (Possible response: His inventions include hair straightener, traffic lights, and the gas mask. He started a newspaper in his community and ran for city council.)

2. **What do you think is the most important thing Garrett Morgan invented?** (Responses will vary.)

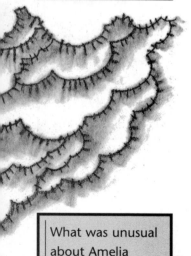

Amelia Earhart

(1897–1937?)

by Jean Marzollo

PURPOSE FOR LISTENING: to gain information

READ-ALOUD TIP: Emphasize each of the "firsts" in Amelia Earhart's life.

She was a daring airplane pilot.

Amelia Earhart was born in Atchison, Kansas. When she grew up, she became a nurse. She nursed wounded soldiers in World War I and went on to study at Columbia University. But Amelia found that she didn't want to be a nurse or a university student. She wanted to become an airplane pilot.

Have students set a purpose for listening.

Her dream surprised people. Airplanes had been invented around the time she was born. They were new and dangerous. Only the bravest men flew them, and people then did not expect women to try such risky adventures.

Nevertheless, in California, Amelia took a job to pay for flying lessons. She loved the excitement of flying. In 1928, she was the first female to fly as a passenger on a plane across the Atlantic Ocean. Afterwards, Amelia wrote a book that told about the trip. Her book was published by a man named George Putnam. Amelia and George fell in love and were married in 1931.

What was unusual about Amelia Earhart's flights across the Atlantic and across the United States?

In 1932, Amelia Earhart flew across the Atlantic Ocean by herself. She was the first woman ever to do this. The trip took about 15 hours. Today, in a modern plane, the same trip would take about five hours. Amelia made other "first woman" trips, too. She flew solo from Hawaii to California and across the United States, first one way and then the other.

Amelia Earhart was a pilot who loved to challenge herself. Her next goal was to be the first woman to fly around the world.

In 1937, she and her co-pilot Fred Noonan began the trip. Unfortunately, they didn't make it. Amelia Earhart's plane was lost near New Guinea in the Pacific Ocean. No one has ever found any traces of Amelia or her plane, but people continue to search for them.

Why did she try such a daring flight? Amelia Earhart once explained her feelings by saying, "Adventure is worthwhile in itself."

---

1. **Do you agree that "adventure is worthwhile in itself"? Explain.** (Responses will vary.)

2. **Amelia Earhart wanted to keep challenging herself. What was her final challenge?** (Possible response: She wanted to be the first woman to fly around the world.)

Figuring Out What's on Your Pet's Mind

by Tracey Randinelli

PURPOSE FOR LISTENING: to gain information

READ-ALOUD TIP: Tell students that this selection is an article from the magazine *Contact Kids.*

Carol Stark says she can tell when her dog Chauncey wants attention. Chauncey, a four-year-old golden retriever, will pick some trash out of a garbage can. "Then," says Carol, "she prances around the living room like she's saying, 'Look what I have.' She does it even though she knows she's not supposed to."

> Do you have pets? If so, how do they try to communicate with you?

Carol isn't the only pet owner who believes her pet's actions communicate its feelings. There are whole books that describe the meaning of animal body language. They claim if the animal's tail is up, for example, the critter is showing a certain feeling. If its ears are down, it's showing a different feeling.

But can you really know for sure what your pets are telling you? Not all pet experts think so. Dr. Linda Goodloe is an animal behaviorist in New York City. According to Goodloe, animals' actions don't always speak louder than words.

For example, most people assume that when a dog's tail is up, it's in a friendly mood. But many dogs don't raise their tails that high to begin with. "If it's a dog that's a little more submissive," says Goodloe, "the tail may wag, but it may be a little lower. You can't say that the tail up means it's friendly. It often is, but not always."

> *Submissive* means "willing to do what someone else wants."

Cats can also be misunderstood. Most people think a cat is happy when it purrs. Cats do purr when they're content. But they may also purr when they're in pain.

And like people, animals may feel more than one emotion at a time. "A dog may be curious and want to greet you, but also a little fearful," says Goodloe. "Even if its tail is wagging, you could get bitten. You have to look at the situation and the individual dog."

Getting Emotional

Many pet owners are certain their pet can tell how they're feeling, too. "If I'm sad," Carol told *Contact Kids*, "Chauncey comes over to me and looks into my eyes as if to say, 'It's okay.'"

But according to Goodloe, pets don't have the ability to pick up on our emotions as much as we think. That's because animals aren't able to show the kinds of emotions people have. "People seem to need to believe that this mental connection exists," Goodloe says. "But the person may be reading something in the behavior that isn't there."

In fact, your pet may not treat you much differently than it would another human—or another dog or cat. "Dogs that want to play do a bow with their front paws down," says Goodloe. "They'll do that with a cat, with a human or with another dog. If cats are feeling comfortable, they'll greet you with their tail in the air and rub against you. They'll do that to anyone if they feel that comfort level."

Carol has seen that kind of behavior in Chauncey. "If I go toward her on all fours and put my head down," she says, "she'll play rougher, like she's playing with another dog."

All in the Past

To understand how your pet communicates, it helps to know something about its ancestors. Take dogs. They are related to wolves. Wolves hunt and hang out in packs. In a group, wolves have a pecking order. Wolves let themselves be pushed around by a more dominant wolf.

Dogs act a lot like wolves. They like to be part of a family—including your family. If your dog howls when you leave him alone, it isn't necessarily feeling sad that you're not there. It may be saying, "I've been separated from the pack. I have to howl to let them know where I am."

A dog also accepts its owner as "top dog." Much of what it communicates is that you are boss. This is usually why a dog won't meet its master's eyes and why it rolls over and shows its belly, swallows or cringes.

> Why can't pets understand our emotions the way people do?

> How are dogs like wolves?

Pack animals have to be able to get their point across to others in their group. That's why dogs are very expressive. Cats, on the other hand, are more solitary. They don't have the same large "vocabulary" as dogs. That means they're harder to figure out.

So how do you communicate with your pet? The best way is to remember it's an animal—not a small human friend. "Learn how animals look at the world," advises Dr. Goodloe. "They don't see or hear the same things." When you see things through your pet's eyes, you'll really understand what it's saying.

> Which kind of animal is harder to understand—a dog or a cat? Why?

1. **What advice does the article give on how to communicate with your pet?** (Possible response: Try to see things through your pet's eyes.)

2. **After reading the information in this article, would you prefer a dog or a cat as a pet? Why?** (Responses will vary.)

Index of Titles and Authors

Themes — Selections	Self Discovery	Working Together	Growth and Change	Creativity	Communities	Explorations	Achievements	Adventures	Animals	Celebrations	Challenges	Courage	Discoveries	Dreams	Families and Friends	Goals	Heroes	Home	Journeys	The Ocean	Plants	The Spirit of America	Tales from Around the World	Timeless Tales
						Collections Themes								**Other Popular Themes**										
Amelia Earhart						•	•	•			•	•				•	•		•			•		
America, the Beautiful Home of Dinosaurs			•						•										•					
Atalanta	•						•				•					•	•	•					•	
Aurora Means Dawn						•	•	•			•	•		•	•			•	•			•		
Bat, The			•						•														•	
Big Moon Tortilla	•										•				•									
Billion Baseballs, A			•								•													
Billy Goat and the Vegetable Garden, The		•							•		•												•	
Clever Turtle, The			•								•												•	
Clever Warthog, The			•								•												•	
Country Mouse and the City Mouse, The	•										•				•			•	•				•	
De Koven						•								•										
Doing Dishes	•										•								•				•	
Eagle Has Landed, The						•	•				•	•	•	•		•	•	•				•		
Figuring Out What's on Your Pet's Mind		•							•				•											
Fish, Flowers, and Fruit				•									•							•	•		•	
Garrett A. Morgan			•				•						•	•										
Good Company			•							•			•											
Half-Chicken		•							•	•									•				•	
Helping		•													•									
How the Girl Taught the Coyotes to Sing Harmony		•					•		•		•												•	
Johnny Appleseed		•					•	•		•	•						•							•
Key of the Kingdom, The			•											•										
Koko's Story		•							•		•				•									
Limericks		•									•								•					

Themes

Selections	Self Discovery	Working Together	Growth and Change	Creativity	Communities	Explorations	Achievements	Adventures	Animals	Celebrations	Challenges	Courage	Discoveries	Dreams	Families and Friends	Goals	Heroes	Home	Journeys	The Ocean	Plants	The Spirit of America	Tales from Around the World	Timeless Tales
Margaret of New Orleans	•						•				•				•		•	•						
Measure of Spice, A				•			•																	
Microscope, The						•	•				•		•										•	
Nine Gold Medals		•					•				•	•		•		•								
Old Crocodile					•				•															
One Little Can					•		•																	
Power Shovel, The			•				•		•		•													
Rudolph Is Tired of the City					•									•					•					
Saturday Night at the Dinosaur Stomp				•							•	•			•									
Scrap and a Robe, A	•						•								•								•	
Since Hanna Moved Away			•				•																	
Someplace Else	•							•							•		•	•						
Take Me Out to the Ball Game		•													•									•
Teddy's Bear					•						•		•									•		
Theft of a Smell, The					•																		•	
Thing That Bothered Farmer Brown, The					•						•													
Three Little Pigs, The		•		•							•				•								•	•
Where Go the Boats?						•		•						•					•					
Why Birds Are Never Hungry		•									•								•				•	